Hospitality with a Heart

Concepts and Models
for Service-Learning in
Lodging, Foodservice,
and **Tourism**

Joseph Koppel, Raphael R. Kavanaugh, and Tom Van Dyke, volume editors

Edward Zlotkowski, series editor

I

Acknowledgment

The support of the American Hotel & Lodging Educational Foundation (www.ahlef.org) and the National Restaurant Association Educational Foundation (www.nraef.org) made this publication possible.

AAHE is an independent, membership-based, nonprofit organization dedicated to building human capital for higher education. AAHE is the source of choice for information about higher education on issues that matter in a democratic, multi-racial society. AAHE members are a national talent pool willing and ready to share their expertise with colleagues in higher education, policymakers, media professionals, and the public at large.

Campus Compact is a national coalition of more than 900 college and university presidents committed to the civic purposes of higher education. To support this civic mission, Campus Compact promotes community service that develops students' citizenship skills and values, encourages partnerships between campuses and communities, and assists faculty who seek to integrate public and community engagement into to their teaching and research. For information about Campus Compact, its services and programs, and publications, go to www.compact.org.

Campus Compact

About this Publication

This volume is the 20th in the AAHE and Campus Compact Series on Service-Learning in the Disciplines. The series editor has been Edward Zlotkowski. Additional copies of this volume, others in the series, the entire set of service-learning volumes, or other AAHE publications may be ordered online at www.aahe.org or by calling AAHE at (800) 504-AAHE (2243). Bulk orders are offered at a discount.

Opinions expressed in this publication are the authors' and do not necessarily represent the views of the American Association for Higher Education, its members, or Campus Compact.

Recommended Bibliographic Listing

Koppel, J., Kavanaugh, R. R., & Van Dyke, T. (2004). *Hospitality with a heart: Concepts and models for service-learning in lodging, foodservice, and tourism.* Washington, DC: American Association for Higher Education.

Editorial Services by QED Associates

10 9 8 7 6 5 4 3 2 1

ISBN: 1-56377-069-5
ISBN (set): 1-56377-005-9

Contents

About This Series

by Edward Zlotkowski

The following volume, *Hospitality with a Heart: Concepts and Models for Service-Learning in Lodging, Foodservice, and Tourism,* is the 20th in a series of monographs on service-learning and the academic disciplines. Ever since the early 1990s, educators interested in reconnecting higher education not only with neighboring communities but also with the American tradition of education for service have recognized the critical importance of winning faculty support for this work. Faculty, however, tend to define themselves and their responsibilities largely in terms of the academic disciplines and interdisciplinary areas in which they have been trained. Hence, the logic of the present series.

The idea for this series first surfaced late in 1994 at a meeting convened by Campus Compact to explore the feasibility of developing a national network of service-learning educators. At that meeting, it quickly became clear that some of those assembled saw the primary value of such a network in its ability to provide concrete resources to faculty working in or wishing to explore service-learning. One resource would be a series of texts on service-learning in a variety of academic disciplines. As this idea began to gain momentum, the American Association for Higher Education, with the encouragement of then vice-president Lou Albert, stepped in to provide critical assistance. Thanks to its reputation for innovative work, AAHE was not only able to obtain the funding needed to support the project up through actual publication, it was also able to assist in attracting many of the teacher-scholars who participated in the project as writers and editors.

The Rationale Behind the Series

A few words should be said at this point about the makeup of both the series and the individual volumes. To some, lodging, foodservice, and tourism may seem a natural choice of academic area with which to link service-learning, since it is largely concerned with questions of providing service to others. "Natural fit," however, was not the determinant in deciding which disciplines and interdisciplinary areas the original series should include. Far more important were considerations related to the overall range of disciplines represented. Since experience has shown that there is probably no disciplinary area — from architecture to zoology — where service-learning cannot be fruitfully employed to strengthen students' abilities to become active learners as well as responsible community members, a primary goal of the original series was to demonstrate this fact. This volume on lodging, foodservice, and tourism, regardless of its "fit," owes its development primarily to the vision and tenacity of its editors. It was they who were determined to demonstrate that, for their discipline, service-learning can be a powerful, indeed transformative, educational force.

Like its predecessors, the present volume has been designed to include its own appropriate theoretical, pedagogical, and bibliographical material. Also like them, it is not meant to provide an extended introduction to service-learning *as a generic concept*. For material of this nature, the reader is referred to such texts as Kendall's *Combining Service and Learning: A Resource Book for Community and Public Service* (NSEE 1990) and Jacoby's *Service-Learning in Higher Education* (Jossey-Bass 1996).

In conclusion, I would like to thank the American Hotel & Lodging Educational Foundation and the National Restaurant Association Educational Foundation for supporting the writing and production of this volume. Working with Michelle Poinelli of the AH&LEF and Mary M. Adolf of the NRAEF, and with the volume editors, has been a pleasure from start to finish.

April 2004

Introduction

by Joseph Koppel

Life is service. The one who progresses is the one who gives his fellow human beings a little more, a little better service.
— Ellsworth Statler

Industry, Education, and Service

Ellsworth Statler (1863-1928) made this statement (Miller 1968: 140) in reference to the service offered his hotel guests, but it would also appear to capture a vision the hospitality industry shares with its program partners in higher education. This monograph will give the reader numerous examples of how the hospitality industry is involved with service to the local community — an involvement providing the perfect backdrop for the many programs that illustrate how hospitality educators are training students to continue the tradition of "civic professionalism" (Sullivan 1996).

Central to the success of the educational programs presented here is a teaching method called service-learning. Thanks to this approach, we can envision a new alliance that would synergize the service efforts of both the hospitality industry and hospitality education. Hence, this volume also serves as a call to align these two separate service efforts for the greater good. A basic plan for this alignment is presented at the end of this volume.

Education for the lodging, foodservice, and tourism industries is an unorthodox discipline within academia. We select from the arts, sciences, and business disciplines and apply them to a major industry. Our professional organization, the Council on Hotel, Restaurant and Institutional Education (CHRIE), was founded in 1946 (Breithaupt 1972), and its growing international membership has resulted in a new acronym: I-CHRIE. From the start, it has enjoyed strong, continuous, and generous support from the industry, its leadership associations, and foundations. Two major foundations (the American Hotel & Lodging Educational Foundation and the National Restaurant Association Educational Foundation) have sponsored the present monograph.

Ellsworth Statler, generally recognized as the father of the modern hotel industry, was also *the* pioneer philanthropist for hotel and restaurant education (Baird 2002). He, and subsequently his foundation, contributed to the development of the first two hotel and restaurant university programs, at Cornell and Michigan State. It was at the former that he established the first practice hotel, Statler Hall.

At the latter, another project he supported, the Kellogg Continuing Education Conference Center, eventually became known as the country's largest laboratory for hotel and restaurant training. Later, his generosity would also result in the first hotel and restaurant program at the two-year-college level, at City College of San Francisco.

Statler's own formal schooling ended in the second grade, but he clearly valued education. He was convinced that the success of the industry would depend on the quality of its training and educational programs. Perhaps the single most important moment in hospitality education occurred when he attended the second annual Hotel Ezra Cornell weekend, a student-run event, in 1927. Arriving on campus, he was initially skeptical about America's first hotel and restaurant educational program, founded in 1922. Until then he believed that individuals interested in a hospitality career would be better served by on-the-job-training, as he had been. By the end of the weekend, however, he was so impressed with what he saw that when asked to say a few words at the closing banquet he confessed: "I'm converted. Meek [professor and founder of the Cornell program] can have any damn thing he wants." Thus, industry support for hospitality education was launched.

If Statler's statement of support can be seen as a critical moment in the early development of hospitality management, the rise of service-learning as a teaching and learning strategy should be considered another such critical moment. Given the fact that service — both as a value and a practice — lies at the core of our discipline, service-learning and hospitality management form a natural pair. It is not surprising, then, that so many academic programs are beginning to develop exciting service-learning courses. Before we review the materials included in this book, it is important to clarify what service-learning is — and what it is not!

Service-Learning Defined

Service-learning is frequently misunderstood or confused with other educational practices. Many mistake it for traditional experiential education. While service-learning is indeed a form of experiential education, it differs by connecting the activity at hand to civic engagement. In addition, it includes still other features as described below.

Each of the essays featured in this monograph reveals different nuances in the approach to community engagement. In the hospitality management program that I founded at the University of San Francisco, I stressed the importance of a planned, systematic integration of classroom and community for their mutual benefit. In the call for papers that launched this volume, the editors used the American Association for Higher Education's definition (cited in my essay below). Ideally, service-learning should exhibit most, if not all, of the following components:

- Attention to the intellectual and civic engagement of students, faculty, and occasionally community staff
- A mutually agreed-upon project that addresses real-world problems faced by a community or a community-based organization (CBO)
- A link between the community problems to be addressed and course content
- Understanding of the conditions that create community problems and how the student service project can change them
- Outcomes and results shared with the community or community organization

It is just as important to note what service-learning is *not* — especially since one of the foundations of effective hospitality programs is required work experience. (Traditionally, two-year programs require 400 hours of structured work experience in industry jobs, while four-year schools require 800 hours or the equivalent of two summers of work experience.) Important as such preprofessional experience is, it is seldom designed to provide broad community benefit and hence does not readily serve as a vehicle of civic awareness.

Extracurricular volunteer activities must also be distinguished from curricular service-learning, for while the former result in "good deeds" they do not necessarily provide deeper learning. For example, I remember when the University of San Francisco received a call for volunteers to help clean up Golden Gate Park. On a Saturday morning, students, faculty, and professional staff worked together to clear wind-damaged areas of the park. Afterwards, participants met for an informal lunch on campus and then quickly dispersed.

A comparison of the rather casual, nonreflective nature of this activity with most of the projects presented in the following essays will suggest the gap that exists between voluntarism and service-learning. Nevertheless, voluntarism clearly plays an important role in our profession, and so we have included an example that illustrates some of the ways in which hospitality education and the hospitality industry can collaborate to address important public needs. This noncurricular essay is located just before the Afterword.

Volume Overview

The table below provides a quick guide to the book's chapters, each of which is identified by institution and the first author. It also has columns to suggest the academic level for which the chapter is most useful.

Academic Level of Essay (Prepared by Tom Van Dyke)

Institution and author	Introductory course	Upper-level course	Independent study	Internship	University program
Johnson & Wales *Connery*		X		X	X
Delaware *Cummings*		X			X
Cornell *O'Connor*		X			
Memphis State *O'Halloran*		X			
Washington State *Swanger*	X				
New Mexico State *Mandabach*	X	X			
San Francisco *Koppel*	X	X			
North Dakota State *Markey*		X			
Indiana U. of Pennsylvania *Van Dyke*		X			
Purdue (Oklahoma State) *Kavanaugh*			X		

In our first chapter, Susan J. Connery, Corrie Martin, and Nancy C. Northrop Wolanski of Johnson & Wales University illustrate how a university known for its hospitality program envisions its contemporary role. The civic engagement movement fueled by Campus Compact and other influential organizations has encouraged colleges and universities to reconnect to higher education's historic mandate to develop an ethos of civic leadership among students. Johnson & Wales is a private, fully accredited university with programs in hospitality, foodservice, technology, and business. The university views its civic mission, to equip students to "become contributing members of society," as a strong complement to its career focus. The authors describe how service-learning has been incorporated into a variety of levels in the curriculum. The success of Johnson & Wales's program has been recognized through both local and regional awards. Service-learning has been a win-win situation for the students, the university, and the community.

In a chapter that helps define service-learning, Pamela Cummings and Ronald P. Cole of the University of Delaware and James A. Myers of the Rochester Institute of Technology explore what they call "*professional* service-learning" (emphasis added), as it relates to hospitality-management education, and they encourage its widespread adoption. Professional service-learning includes planned activities where hospitality-course students apply content-specific information and managerial skill-building activities to problems or situations in real community settings. The authors identify a wide variety of service-learning activities available to hospitality programs. They also describe the annual meeting students have designed, planned, and executed for the Food Bank of Delaware. This event has been so successful that the Hotel, Restaurant and Institutional Management (HRIM) program at the University of Delaware has changed its mission statement to include service-learning as one of four primary educational goals.

Next, Therese A. O'Connor and Stephanie Rainsford of Cornell University, along with Marge Dill and Nancy Burston of the Human Services Coalition of Tompkins County, New York, challenge educators to think out of the box. Traditional service-learning courses have students work primarily at nonprofit organizations. O'Connor et al. envision a more complex collaboration between for-profit hospitality businesses and nonprofit organizations, with hospitality students acting as liaisons between the two. After describing a course entitled Housing and Feeding the Homeless, the authors analyze postsemester surveys of the course and some of the students' concerns. They then suggest exciting hypothetical scenarios or potential service-learning projects, involving students in organized learning situations with for-profit businesses that would also benefit nonprofit organizations, advance the students' education, and strengthen the community.

Robert M. O'Halloran and Cynthia S. Deale of Memphis State University present a very convincing list of benefits that students derive from service-learning activities. They also provide valuable project profiles as a resource for hospitality educators. One example involves college students teaching nutrition to public-school children. Another involves a "Kids' Cuisine" project in which students designed, created, and tested children's menu items with elementary school students. A third project, "Think Like an Owner," helped contribute to economic development plans, as students examined possibilities for revitalizing a town's waterfront.

Not all projects need be so ambitious. Service-learning can also be used in an introductory course. Nancy Swanger of Washington State University describes her fall 2001 project as it evolved over the course of the semester. After discussing its design and grading system, she shares some of her students' feedback. Swanger explicitly differentiates between traditional service and service-learning, and concludes with a description of the changes planned for the course's next iteration.

On the culinary side, Keith H. Mandabach of New Mexico State University discusses how service-learning activities enable students to improve their technical skills, develop pride in their profession, and reflect on the connection between student effort and community well-being. He traces the move from volunteerism to service-learning in foodservice education, to clarify some of the differences between them, and discusses the philosophical foundations of service-learning.

The next chapter is mine, written as an associate professor of hospitality at the University of San Francisco. It develops some of the areas that Malcolm Knowles discussed in his work on andragogy, an adult- or student-centered concept of education. The chapter describes how service-learning was used in a beverage management/wine-tasting course; in another course, Introduction to Hospitality Management, students developed their skills and awareness while working with a foodservice job-training program for the homeless.

The many ways in which service-learning enhances the hospitality curriculum are the focus of a chapter by Vern Markey of North Dakota State University and Pamela Holsinger-Fuchs of the University of Minnesota-Crookston. When students work on projects with local residents and leaders, they are exposed to issues such as economics, demographics, state and local political systems, and environmental resource management. The authors describe how a food-service administration class was given the task of developing cyclical menus for a nonprofit, long-term-care facility located in a small town in Minnesota and a homeless shelter. They also discuss how they applied service-learning in a global tourism course.

Service-learning can also be applied in senior capstone courses. Tom Van Dyke of Indiana University of Pennsylvania challenges his students to do projects for community organizations that lack resources to meet their needs. The students experience the true nature of poverty when representatives from community-service organizations speak to their class, and when they work with those organizations. The students, whose assignments include a presentation on some aspect of hunger or homelessness, also are encouraged to become advocates for those in need by writing letters to elected officials.

Finally, Raphael R. Kavanaugh of Purdue University explores how students exposed to service-learning can learn to recognize the importance of improving the quality of life for those less fortunate, realize their own potential as problem-solvers, and appreciate their role as active citizens in their community. Kavanaugh then describes how the Oklahoma Restaurant Association, together with hotel and restaurant administration students from Oklahoma State University, responded to the Oklahoma City bombing. Although their response is an example of community service rather than service-learning, Kavanaugh discusses how colleges and universities can turn experiences like this one into service-learning. He also challenges I-CHRIE members to consider service-learning as a vehicle to stimulate economic development — an ambitious strategy to promote the well-being of our communities.

The Afterword explores the many ways in which *both* hospitality educators and industry leaders are contributing to the greater community and working toward the common good. Why, then, are these two groups not working more in common? We have an opportunity to link two strong traditions in addressing today's community needs and thus achieve even more than we can accomplish working separately. It is, in short, time for I-CHRIE to seek a new type of partnership with its industry colleagues. It is time for us to become true Partners in Service.

The volume concludes with an annotated bibliography by Keith H. Mandabach. Here the reader will find valuable additional information about linking community-based work and hospitality education.

Acknowledgments

This publication would not exist without the endorsement of I-CHRIE's 1998 Board of Directors, and particularly Raphael Kavanaugh's initial encouragement. In addition, all I-CHRIE members need to express deep gratitude for the foresight and generosity of our ever-supportive partners in education, the American Hotel & Lodging Educational Foundation and the National Restaurant Association Educational Foundation. Both Michelle Poinelli of the AH&LEF and Mary M. Adolf of the NRAEF have been most encouraging of this effort. Special thanks are owed also to my co-editors, Raphael Kavanaugh, who managed external relations and funding, and Tom Van Dyke, who contributed significantly to the "Volume Overview" section, above, and chaired the volume's editorial review committee, whose members were Alice Kaiser-Drobney, Dori Finley, Tom, and I. Editing assistance was provided by Shelley Weaver. On behalf of my co-editors, I extend the warmest appreciation to our students, whose commitment both to this project and our discipline have inspired us all.

One last professional expression of gratitude is for our series editor, Edward Zlotkowski. He makes being hospitable so easy. His knowledge and passion of service-learning are so contagious. Over a dinner in San Francisco he invited our discipline "to the table." We in hospitality education owe a debt of gratitude to him and to the American Association for Higher Education for this opportunity. Thank you, Edward, Campus Compact, and AAHE, for all your guidance and encouragement.

The process of creating this volume provided an opportunity for our discipline, which has often been regarded as an academic stepchild, to stand with other major academic fields that are a part of this series. This publication, it is hoped, will help establish our credibility to the academy and make our colleagues more aware of an important teaching method that combines learning with social activism.

References

Baird, Cathleen. (2002). www.uh.edu.hallofhonor.

Breithaupt, Herman A. (1972). "Then Came the Formation of CHRIE." In *How We Started Students on Successful Foodservice Careers: Chef Herman's Story*. Edited by Jane Wilkinson, 54-58. Chicago, IL: Institutions/Volume Feeding Magazine.

Miller, Floyd. (1968). *America's Extraordinary Hotelman: Statler*. New York: The Statler Foundation.

Sullivan, William. (1996). *Work and Integrity*. New York: Harper Business.

It's Not *either* Be Involved *or* Look at the Bottom Line: Developing Hospitality Students into Community and Industry Leaders in a Post-September 11 World

by Susan J. Connery, Corrie Martin, and Nancy C. Northrop Wolanski

Before September 11 made the whole nation revisit its priorities, the hospitality industry had begun to embrace a more concrete sense of social responsibility, with indicators that leaders in many sectors were examining the larger impact and civic purposes of their business. The restaurant field, too, saw a new community awareness developing, exemplified by the National Restaurant Association's (comprising more than 844,000 restaurant and foodservice outlets and 11.3 million employees) launch of a "comprehensive effort to advance and promote the restaurant industry's role as a cornerstone of community involvement, career and employment opportunities and the economy" (Hospitality Net 2002a).

As the industry began to change and recognize civic goals, the schools and colleges responsible for educating the next generation of hospitality leaders were also being challenged to embody civic values. The civic engagement movement fueled by Campus Compact and other influential organizations encouraged colleges and universities to reconnect to higher education's historic mandate to develop an ethos of civic leadership among students.

September 11 Turning Points

September 11 caused many organizations, industries, and individuals to revisit these important questions of citizenship, responsibility, values, and community impact. Much of the nation has experienced a resurgence in community awareness and an increased interest in community involvement since 9/11, as citizens have sought solace, comfort, and meaning in a renewed commitment and connection to neighbors, community-based organizations, and family. The hospitality industry, however, also finds itself pulled in another direction. The crippling economic implications of the terrorist attack have forced many employers in the industry to cut staff, streamline operations, and focus on reviving the bottom line. These threadbare times seem to require cold-hearted business decisions far removed from the altruistic heroism displayed and embodied by many in the hospitality industry in the days and weeks following the attack. A study released in November 2002 warned that two million jobs in hotels, rental-car agencies, convention centers, theme parks, restaurants, and travel agencies would be lost over a 16-month period following the attacks (Hospitality Net 2002b).

The hospitality industry stands at a challenging crossroads. Can "community involvement" endure, and even thrive, in an industry reeling from a difficult economy? Can social responsibility coexist with, and even enhance, business performance and profit? Are there win-win opportunities for the industry and the communities in which hospitality companies do business?

These questions also create a ripple effect for the higher-education institutions training the hospitality workforce. Can civic engagement and community leadership be combined with business savvy, management skills, and hands-on training to create a new kind of leader in the hospitality industry? Can today's students wholeheartedly pursue a career in the hospitality industry while not "selling out" to insular, profit-driven individualism?

Johnson & Wales University, one of the leading hospitality educators in the country, offers a promising case study in the opportunities to merge the seemingly divergent balance sheets of profitability and community into a bottom line that pays off for companies, employees, and communities.

Johnson & Wales University: Career and Community

Johnson & Wales University (J&W) is uniquely positioned to address these questions because of its distinctive mission and history, which combine an acute awareness of and focus on industry with a long-term commitment to community leadership. Known as "America's Career University," J&W is a private, nonprofit, fully accredited university of more than 13,000 students with campuses located in Providence, Denver, North Miami, Charleston, and Norfolk, and education programs in hospitality, foodservice, technology, and business. It offers associate's and bachelor's degrees from three colleges: culinary arts, business, and hospitality. Graduate programs include an MBA with concentrations in organizational management, international business, accounting, and hospitality administration; an MAT in foodservice education and business education (with or without certification); and a Ph.D. in educational leadership.

Johnson & Wales takes the term "career university" very seriously, measuring its success each year on the basis of the job placement rate of its graduates. In order to maintain the 98-percent placement rate it has had for many years, J&W has developed a unique, career-focused curriculum that integrates theoretical and academic training with hands-on exposure and real-life experience. Students not only learn specific professional skills but also gain valuable field experience while earning their degrees. The skills highlighted in the curriculum are determined through the DACUM (Developing A CurriculUM) process, in which industry representatives are asked to identify necessary skills for different positions in their organizations. That feedback is then used to revise and focus the curriculum, so that J&W graduates are prepared with the skills to succeed in any given industry. This emphasis on career education and industry involvement ensures J&W's sensitivity to marketplace concerns. It also influences the administrative structure of the university, which often resembles an entrepreneurial corporation more than a typical educational bureaucracy. In accrediting J&W, the New England Association of Schools & Colleges concluded that its "focus on students, their education and their career readiness is an extraordinary strength of Johnson & Wales University and pervades virtually every element of the University."

Johnson & Wales's career mission (to equip students to "achieve success in employment fields with high growth potential") would seem to put the university at odds with the traditional public service mission of higher education. Since all university programs and plans are sifted through a career sieve, it would seem that civic and community concerns might be regarded as chaff, to be discarded on the way to successful career development. But, since its inception, the university has seen its civic mission, to equip students to "become contributing members of society," as a strong complement to its career focus. The initiatives of the Hospitality College have demonstrated this over the last decade.

J&W Hospitality College Early Community Initiatives

Through a grant from the CARLISLE Foundation of Framingham, Massachusetts, J&W was able to hire a full-time director in 1993 to work in the J&W Practicum Education Office and develop opportunities for Hotel and Culinary Internship students to use their skills to address issues of hunger and homelessness. The internship program sought to create a profitable educational partnership that both assisted nonprofits in their drive to eliminate hunger in Rhode Island and fulfilled the university's mission of developing students with the professional and personal qualities to be leaders in their field. In 1993, a service-learning rotation at the Rhode Island Community Food Bank was integrated into the Hotel Internship program, and in the following year the Culinary Forum, working with four emergency food-distribution sites, was instituted for Culinary Internship students.

Community Service-Learning (CSL) was integrated into students' internship experience because it was clearly a strong opportunity for gaining hands-on career experience in growth-producing settings. Students in the Hotel-Restaurant Management, Food and Beverage Management, Culinary Arts, and Pastry Arts Programs spend a term rotating through different on-campus food-related sites, including dining halls, à la carte restaurants, and banquet facilities, gaining practical, first-hand experience in a variety of culinary and hospitality settings. One rotation required for all practicum students, since the early 1990s, is a week-long Community Service Practicum, taught by staff and graduate students from J&W's Alan Shawn Feinstein Community Service Center. Each week, the program introduces 12-16 culinary and 10-15 hospitality students to social responsibility concepts and specific opportunities within the culinary and hospitality industries, to address issues of hunger and homelessness.

On the first day, students attend a three-hour lecture on the systemic issues surrounding hunger, food insecurity, and poverty, and are challenged to identify ways that, as professionals in the hospitality industry, they will be able to address some of these community needs. On days two through four, the students prepare and serve meals at emergency meal sites, the statewide food bank, and eldercare facilities, to learn about food redistribution, nutritional needs of at-risk populations, and creative use of limited resources. (Current sites include the Rhode Island Community Food Bank, Amos House, Travelers Aid Society of Rhode Island, St. Charles' Soup Kitchen, McAuley House, and senior centers.) Students then take an exam on the poverty and hunger statistics covered in the lecture, and also complete a written assignment that includes a case study in which they develop a plan for their future involvement in the community as hotel or restaurant managers.

Benefits of Community Involvement

The public benefits of integrating community placements into job preparation programs are obvious: such programs provide energetic and skilled assistance to nonprofits that are chronically short-staffed and underfunded. Since 1994, students in the Community Service Practicum have prepared 216,000 meals for Food Bank network agencies in the Food Bank demo kitchen, keeping the cost to $.50 per meal. This amounts to 19,152 hours of student labor (approximately $95,760 in saved labor costs for the Food Bank). Hospitality Practicum students have given 6,638 hours to salvaging efforts (representing $33,190 in saved labor costs), maximizing the number of meals that can be processed by the Prepared & Perishable Food Rescue and

Community Kitchen programs. By increasing food production and efficiency, J&W has helped the Food Bank to stretch dollars to feed more people.

Public-relations dividends for the sponsoring organization are also fairly evident. The Providence campus of J&W, a large, private, landholding, nonprofit (and therefore non-taxpaying) institution, had an uneasy relationship with the city until the early 1990s, when the university made a public commitment to invest in the growth and revitalization of the city. Visible community partnerships and the influx of thousands of student volunteers every year have contributed to a greatly improved relationship with the city and an increasingly positive public perception of the university.

Less obvious, however, are the long-term benefits to students and to the hospitality industry.

Community Involvement as a Skill-Development Opportunity

Beyond encouraging student versatility and development through the application of curricular skills in new settings (often under challenging circumstances, with limited resources and supervision), J&W seeks to deepen students' service experiences, so that they are not only using traditional skills but developing new ones. Under the rubric of community leadership, students learn principles of social responsibility, civic engagement, and corporate citizenship through which they learn how to identify community needs, match available resources, and participate in collaborative initiatives and action. This simple approach can be easily transferred to any professional context, since the skills required (including needs assessment, critical thinking, resource development and allocation, teamwork, collaborative problem solving, ability to work with diverse groups and individuals, and ongoing evaluation) are essential for any manager in the hospitality industry.

The recognition of the overlap between civic and career skills is the foundation of J&W's CSL program, which, in 1995, became a graduation requirement for all undergraduates, thanks to an endowment given by the Feinstein Foundation. The Feinstein "Enriching America" Program requires students to complete both theoretical and experiential CSL components. The mandatory, introductory 10-hour course in service-learning theory, SL1001, was developed to prepare students for community involvement and give them a framework in which to process the CSL experiential component. Shortly after the program began, more than 755 students participated in SL1001, and more than 50 faculty members partnered with 110 nonprofit agencies to offer service experiences related to coursework and designed to give students the opportunity to develop skills, learn to relate to diverse audiences, and apply their knowledge to pressing community concerns.

The CSL program encourages skill development in a variety of ways. Students enrolled in the Hospitality College's four-year bachelor's program in recreation/leisure management spend one term as interns, rotating through a series of hands-on assignments at the university's recreation center, fitness centers, and other venues. In addition, they spend time weekly working at a local Boys & Girls Club (BGC) in a low-income, at-risk neighborhood.

While the BGC experience is valuable in providing another setting for the students to apply their skills, it is even more valuable in challenging them to think creatively about program development and problem solving.

In a thorough orientation, the students, led by a Feinstein Community Service Center staff person and the director of the BGC, work through a variety of exercises designed both to increase their ownership and understanding of the important role they play at the BGC and also to lay the groundwork for a meaningful relationship that encourages them to think of themselves as more than temporary "volunteers" at the BGC.

After a brief introduction, students are asked to work in pairs to fill out a "Question Generator" worksheet that forms the basis of an informational interview with the director of the BGC. The worksheet is a brainstorming device encompassing four areas: BGC's organizational profile and identity, resources and assets, threats and challenges, and programming. The students are encouraged to learn logistical information about their community site and also to understand the context in which they will do their work. For example, in one session students asked the BGC director the difference between the BGC and YMCA/YWCA, and this question generated an interesting discussion about the social purposes of recreation, accessibility issues, and the ways in which meaningful recreation programs and activities contribute to youth development and family stability. Questions about the demographic profile of children at the BGC have prompted discussions about poverty and its repercussions, while questions about the BGC's history have revealed that Rhode Island hosts the second oldest BGC in the country. Since the interview is based on the students' own questions, they have a stake in the answers and are "hooked" on their site by the end of the session.

A follow-up worksheet entitled "Making Your Connections" builds on the interest and understanding generated by the interview, and thus helps students use the community leadership process both to focus their thinking and to make informed decisions about the projects and activities they choose to become involved in. Interview information about what intrigues them, and an analysis of the reasons for their interest and their experience and talents, helps students identify the resources they bring to their placement, as well as special projects or activities they would like to lead at the BGC. Students also use the worksheet to describe a challenge faced by the club, and to suggest a way in which they might be able to help solve it. By discussing their answers with the BGC's director, they become familiar with needs assessment, resource allocation, problem solving, and critical thinking.

This process not only provides a direction for the service experience but, more importantly, frequently offers students their first solid sense of the broader social responsibilities of their chosen career field. By the end of their placement, they have learned that the recreation/leisure field goes far beyond fun and games; it has a long history of seeking to build community, support impoverished families, and contribute to youth development. Susan Meyer, the director of operations at the Fox Point Boys & Girls Club, site of the 2001-2002 placements, notes two distinct student learning outcomes: "Working at the club, students become so much more aware of their own potential to impact others, how important it is to be conscious of your influence as a role-model, to be patient and understanding with each other. Also, I observe how the students become more attuned to the different facets of the recreation/leisure field by being immersed in the diverse settings of the club."

Leadership Development and Global Perspectives Through Community Involvement

Leaving the classroom and stepping into real-life situations is an important dimension of any experiential education experience. For all of their challenges, CSL placements are uniquely positioned to develop and enhance the leadership and global perspectives of students. Corporate internships are usually in highly structured environments, with a firm chain of command and relatively little room for creativity or new program development. The nonprofit arena, however, is fertile ground for the development of leadership and larger perspectives, because it must deal with staff and resource shortages and is committed to issues affecting different populations.

This ability to take the initiative and to understand the interrelated global factors that affect an industry or specific business is critical to the hospitality industry. Even before September 11, at the first forum held by Business Enterprises for Sustainable Travel (BEST) at the World Travel & Tourism Council in South Africa, 28 of the world's top university-based tourism and hospitality programs agreed "to incorporate . . . modules on sustainable tourism into their own programs [and] develop a vehicle for sharing teaching aids and extending the curriculum to other university and tourism/hospitality training programs around the world" (Hospitality Net 2002c).

Now, in a post-9/11 world, the importance of understanding global perspectives and impacts cannot be overstated. At J&W, the Hospitality College's service-learning activities seek to educate students to see themselves not only as employees of a certain company or private industry but as public professionals who are connected through their careers and workplaces to broader communities and worldwide issues.

At J&W, travel-tourism management students devote one term of their sophomore year to the university's internship program, during which they rotate through various professional sites (a tour operator, a university travel agency, etc.) as well as quasi-governmental and nonprofit sites. Students spend time working at a regional tourism council, a city visitors' bureau, and an information booth run by the state's Department of Economic Development. These experiences provide a hands-on context for understanding the connections between their professional field and the economic life of a city, state, and region. But the connection does not end with the uncritical notion that tourism is good for the economy and hence for people.

As part of the internship curriculum each term, groups of travel-tourism interns plan and execute a tour abroad. Recently, for example, students planned trips to Canada, Brazil and Argentina, and Eastern Europe. Hence, it is important that students understand the global context and impact of their work. At the beginning of the internship, students learn about the complexities of tourism's relationship to poverty and environmental degradation around the globe. They are introduced to the claim that travel-tourism has had a greater global impact on the quality of life and the environment than any other industry since the industrial revolution — as well as to the unique opportunity of future travel-tourism professionals to make a difference through wise and visionary community leadership.

In fall 2002, the Hospitality College piloted a new CSL program designed to enhance the leadership skills and experiences of undergraduate travel-tourism teaching assistants (who have completed the associate's degree and assumed leadership positions in the program) and graduate student assistants, as well as introduce associate's-level travel-tourism students to the interconnectedness of local and global communities through an innovative partnership with a Rhode Island community partner.

The program involves a "travel academy," matching travel-tourism management interns with middle school students enrolled in the new Sophia Academy, a private, nondenominational, nonprofit school for at-risk girls in Providence. The hospitality students mentor the girls in the skills of exploring and understanding the world through travel and research, as well as serve as career and personal role models. Teams of J&W students, facilitated by teaching assistants and graduate assistants, meet with a class of seventh-grade girls every Friday for two hours, teaching them about different aspects of the travel-tourism profession, leading team-building and leadership activities, and seeking to build relationships and self-esteem among the girls. Students from Sophia Academy rarely ever travel beyond their own neighborhood, much less to different parts of the city or state, so the J&W students introduce them to skills involved in planning and organizing trips to local sites. The field trips help the girls get to know their communities, state, and region. The J&W students learn the ways in which different forms and patterns of segregation and self-segregation isolate groups from each other, and how the travel-tourism profession can help to break down those barriers; they also gain an understanding of the clear connection between their career field and significant community and youth issues in Providence. The teaching assistants and graduate assistants learn basic fund development and grant writing while working with resource development and allocation to implement the Travel Academy.

Another aspect of the local and regional focus of these activities is to encourage critical thinking about local connections to global or international issues. Weeks of research and planning go into each student group's overseas trip, and this is shared with the Sophia Academy students as it progresses. Prior to departing for their international city, the students lead the girls through in-depth explorations of the cultural, historical, and geographical details of the destination. In addition, they involve J&W international students from those destination countries, whenever possible.

By using the travel-tourism field to empower the girls to recognize their self-worth and potential for leadership, the J&W students serve as role models for continuing education and professional development. The program includes career development workshops for girls and their parents (most of them single mothers), many of whom are employed in the hospitality industry. Thus, students also learn about the workplace challenges to dignity and respect faced by many in the industry.

"Kicking Up" Civic Education and Community Involvement

One reason why the hospitality industry, among others, may struggle to see the importance of community involvement is that it often regards it as fluff, a feel-good, be-nice approach to life that cannot survive economic downturns. As J&W's most famous alumnus, chef Emeril Lagasse, might say, the hospitality industry would be well served to "kick it up a notch." Johnson & Wales is committed to developing the CSL program beyond civics (which most adults associate with boring lectures on how a bill becomes a law) and beyond citizenship (which most adults limit to participation in the electoral process), to *community leadership*.

The community leadership activities at the Providence campus of J&W target two goals: developing students into community leaders and developing J&W into a community leader in the Providence community (through staff, departmental, and institutional involvement). One essential ingredient that differentiates community leadership from service or volunteerism is: strategy. Community leadership is concerned with impact — first with community impact, which is important in a public-relations context, but perhaps even more so in a sound business context, because investing in the community where one does business ensures a community that will be conducive to doing business successfully and profitably; and second with personal and institutional impact. The forethought that goes into community leadership ensures that resources are used for maximum impact and effectiveness, that all partners receive benefits, and that productive relationships and networks are established.

This leadership component helps set J&W's CSL program apart and ensures its compatibility with the university's career-focused mission. Mere exposure to social issues can be overwhelming if students are not equipped to use their skills and to work with existing resources to make a difference. Since 1994, J&W's John Hazen White School of Arts & Sciences has offered courses and a concentration in leadership studies, a discipline that provides additional tools for students interested in using their skills to effect community change. The Center for Leadership Studies, officially opened in 1997, offers programs that have reinforced the university's service initiatives. Students and staff have been trained to develop their leadership skills and have been challenged to apply them within and outside of the university community. Indeed, recognizing the value of the program, the university has instituted a leadership requirement for graduation. Beginning in 2001-2002, all students in almost all programs are required to take a Foundations of Leadership course. Johnson & Wales's commitment to providing leadership training and targeted service opportunities for all students, instead of a select few, sets the program apart from many other national programs, and this inclusivity has been recognized by national figures in leadership development. As a result, J&W has made community leadership one of the 13 "Vision Points" in Vision 2006, the university's five-year strategic plan, ensuring that the university will continue to prioritize strategic involvement in Providence and other J&W locations.

Kathy Drohan, the director of the Travel-Tourism Internship at J&W, clearly recognizes the potential of community leadership in the Travel Academy project. The academy was designed to drive home to students the importance of community — particularly the interconnectedness of the local and global communities — to the travel-tourism industry, and was structured with community leadership goals in mind. "We wanted to raise the level of what we were doing, from community service to community leadership," she says. "In the past, we've structured into the students' scheduled rotations community-based organizations and the like, but now the students are taking the lead in creating a lasting, mutually rewarding relationship between our school, our profession, and real people who might not have access to these experiences or skills otherwise."

Changing an Industry

For many J&W students, the CSL experience is the first time they have thought about issues of economic disparity or have interacted with people in need. By participating in this experience, they not only continue learning about hospitality-related skills and the community applications of their expertise but also begin to see the wealth of opportunity hidden in the community. As they develop new skills and experiences, such as rescuing food, working with clients from diverse backgrounds, and maximizing limited resources, they come to understand that the community is no longer merely a recipient of their goodwill but an integral part of their own growth and development.

Direct community experience in CSL enables interns to view the industry differently as well. They are assigned to write research papers that discuss the role, scope, philosophy, and definition of community service in their field, and how successful community service might be developed and achieved by different types of hospitality-related companies. Internship experiences give students a new understanding that "service to the community" (after-hours, off-the-clock) is not the final goal, but rather, that genuine and effective community involvement can be an integral part of hospitality education and professionalism. Their experience during the CSL also shows that good management practices often go hand-in-hand with civic involvement, as the students are challenged to think creatively about the role that hotels and restaurants can play in alleviating hunger and addressing issues of poverty. As future leaders in the foodservice and hospitality industries, students get exposure to alternative, socially responsible ways of doing business, and how responsibility often helps the bottom line.

The J&W programs prepare students to thrive in a field notorious for its often exploitative labor practices and historic devaluation of cultural and environmental resources. The programs seek to realize the civic potential of the hospitality profession and the civic identity of its professionals. Business Enterprises for Sustainable Travel (BEST), a group of tourism and travel educators, has identified the key to long-term change in tourism as the ability of professional education programs to go about "mainstreaming sustainable tourism material into the curriculum" (Hospitality Net 2002c). Such mainstreaming, in order to have broad impact upon the hospitality industry for generations to come, should occur through experiential education. Service-learning has powerful and diverse applications in this context, as students begin to form their professional identities and draw immediate connections between what they do and how it affects others. Service-learning programs and projects help students increase their ability to build civic traditions directly into their professional work. Students are encouraged to see their jobs not only as a means to make a living but as an authentic way to create and sustain strong community relationships.

Growth of a Program

The Feinstein "Enriching America" Program at J&W has grown substantially, since 1996, providing more than 1,700 students each year with service-learning experiences through academic modules, practicum programs, community leadership courses, student mentorships, and special projects. Many of the 6,000 students who have completed the experiential CSL commitment at community sites have had their first up-close exposure to social issues in this program, and while they have contributed thousands of hours of service to more than 100 local agencies, they have received even more in terms of personal and professional development and an expanded world view.

In 1999, J&W's Alan Shawn Feinstein Graduate School hired a graduate community service-learning coordinator to integrate project-based service-learning into graduate courses, ensuring that every student, graduate or undergraduate, has a first-hand opportunity to learn about social issues. In the first year of the coordinator's work, almost a third of the graduate students participated in community service-learning projects, and more than 300 were introduced to community service through classroom presentations. Their advanced coursework and expertise have enabled the graduate students to undertake large, complex projects related to their classes, including developing brochures, manuals, and forms; doing research and marketing analysis; and helping eight different nonprofits with public relations.

The success of J&W's program has been recognized through both local and regional awards. In addition, the Feinstein "Enriching America" Program has attracted national attention. As early as 1996, it was the subject of two national articles (*Hope* magazine and an Associated Press story carried in 48 states). In 1997, judges awarded the J&W Community Education Programs a gold medal in the Community Relations Program and Projects category of the CASE Circle of Excellence Awards. Johnson & Wales was one of only three entries receiving an award in this category. In 1999, the program was featured in the *Templeton Guide: Colleges That Encourage Character Development,* one of 60 community service programs chosen to be profiled from a pool of 250 applicants, and one of only 10 that received a top ranking. Finally, the Points of Light Foundation named the Feinstein Center the National Daily Point of Light for March 20, 2001, in recognition of its efforts to engage students in local hunger-relief efforts.

Conclusion

Before September 11, the hospitality industry began acknowledging the importance of integrating into the bottom line such concepts and practices as community and youth development, sustainable business, environmentalism, and long-term employee support. "Based on our research," says Michael Seltzer, who directs the BEST initiative of the World Travel & Tourism Council, "we know many leaders of forward-looking companies that have built successful travel enterprises that contribute to their destination's cultural, social and environmental well-being" (Hospitality Net 2002c). It is a challenge to sustain this focus in a difficult economy, but J&W's hospitality programs, which combine "hard-core" business training and skills with community leadership education and experiences, provide a promising model for transforming the hospitality industry.

Hospitality educators need to take note of recommendations offered by Boyte and Kari, in a 1996 book about the role of public work in a democracy. The authors refer (172) to studies suggesting "that highly successful companies are never simply driven by profit making alone, despite the dogmas of free market economics. For these businesses, making money is part of a complex of values and larger purposes." We in hospitality education need to change our pedagogical mission to reflect this reality, and prepare our students to succeed in a dynamic industry motivated by an ethic of care. As Boyte and Kari suggest (187), our educational mission can go beyond training and narrow professionalism to teaching students how to work with their fellow citizens. Colleges that educate for public work cultivate people's capacities to imagine and to act beyond given frameworks; they teach a tolerance for different voices and ways of knowing; they tie such intellectual traits to the ability to act effectively on important tasks; and they teach people how to discern the larger meaning of their work.

All of this is essential to business — and to community.

References

Boyte, Harry, and Nanci Kari. (1996). *Building Democracy: The Democratic Promise of Public Work*. Philadelphia: Temple University Press.

Hospitality Net. (2002a, May 21). "National Restaurant Association Launches Restaurants of Promise Initiative — Program Concentrates on Helping Young People through Community Activity, Career Mentoring." www.hospitalitynet.org/news/4007987.html.

_____. (2002b, November 22). "The Travel and Tourism Industry Hammered Hard in Wake of September 22 Attack." www.hospitalitynet.org/news/4010241.html.

_____. (2002c, April 5). "Conference Board/Best Global Think Tank Focuses on Travel that Benefits both Community and Environment." www.hospitalitynet.org/news/4007544.html.

Enhanced Professional Socialization Through Service-Learning

by Pamela Cummings, Ronald P. Cole, and James A. Myers

Service-learning is a form of experiential education in which students engage in activities that address human and community needs together with structured opportunities intentionally designed to promote student learning and development. Reflection and reciprocity are key concepts of service-learning.
— Jacoby et al. (1996)

The term service-learning has been defined and redefined over the past few years and has left some confusion in the hospitality education community. If you had asked a professor of hospitality to define service-learning a few years ago, you might have heard something about service quality, the Malcolm Baldrige Award, or the Platinum Rule. Others have seen service-learning as synonymous with altruism, where students plan volunteer activities in classes or, more often, student organizations. A more developed definition might include similar community activities, but planned and coordinated by faculty and relevant to the course that sponsors them. However, even here the emphasis would probably remain on external beneficiaries, that is, community recipients.

The purpose of this chapter is to define "professional service-learning" as it relates to hospitality-management education, and to encourage its adoption. Such professional service-learning includes planned activities in which students apply content-specific hospitality-course information and managerial skill-building activities to problems or dilemmas in community settings. Specifically, faculty and students are involved in various aspects of providing food or hospitality job training for community program participants (Loschert 2001). Thus, the activities of hospitality students represent authentic acts of service, civic contributions, and are genuinely valuable to the recipients. Of equal importance, however, these activities flow from course objectives, which are themselves based both on the developmental needs of the students and on identified community needs. Student learning includes affective and cognitive components, and in its experiential setting is consistent with the philosophy set forth by John Dewey (1938).

The recent growth of service-learning as a pedagogical strategy has been impressive. In fact, service-learning is one of the fastest growing movements in higher education (Howard 2000-2001). This growth may be a response partly to public criticism of the academic community. Several reports published in the 1980s and early 1990s criticized the academy, and several of the charges are relevant to this chapter, such as social isolation and lack of curricular relevance to the local community (Boyer 1988, 1990; Commission for Educational Quality 1985; Bok 1982). Rice (1996) described the academic community as having turned inward, developing knowledge for purposes other than social benefit, with primary allegiance to academic societies, and with intellectual power monopolized by the academy rather than shared with the larger society. This public disengagement of universities has been attributed to various forces, but one of its results has been to de-emphasize the historical civic mission of colleges and universities (Kezar and Rhoads 2001; Lucas 1994).

Service-learning holds the promise of helping restore citizenship education to the academy through community participation by faculty and students, since one of its distinguishing elements is preparation for citizenship (Cameron et al. 2001). Terms such as "civic mandate," "social responsibility," and "larger public good" appear often in descriptions of service-learning programs. According to Checkoway (2001), there is renewed interest in democracy in American higher education and in preparing our students for improving their communities. In national associations, there is new interest in the civic mission of the American research university. Campus Compact, a coalition of more than 800 college and university presidents, and the Campus Opportunity Outreach League (COOL), a student-based organization, are committed to furthering civic engagement (Howard 2001; Kezar and Rhoads 2001). They are part of a reform movement that promotes service-learning, community service, and collaborative partnerships between campuses and their communities. Moving out of the insular community of a campus changes students by broadening their perspectives, raising their awareness, and stimulating them toward political or community advocacy. According to Ernest Boyer, "college succeeds as its graduates are inspired by a larger vision, using the knowledge they have acquired to form values and advance the common good" (1988: 296).

Hospitality Education's Niche in Professional Service-Learning

Incorporating service-learning into a discipline can be a formidable task. Before deciding where to begin or what to do, Enos and Troppe (1996:159) suggest asking the following questions: "What purpose does this discipline serve in society? What does its knowledge base offer ordinary citizens?" For hospitality-management students, this presents an opportunity to use their unique expertise on one of the most serious problems in our communities, our country, and the world: hunger.

Our country is the most affluent nation in the history of the world, and yet 31 million Americans are worried about getting enough to eat. It would be comforting to believe that hunger is a problem of the past, but it persists here and across the world. We have an opportunity to reinforce professional skills, enhance managerial strategies, and foster citizenship and leadership development while helping to relieve hunger. And the best place to begin is in our own communities.

To appreciate the scope of the hunger problem, consider recent data collected by America's Second Harvest (O'Brien and Aldeen 2001):

• Approximately 23.3 million low-income Americans seek emergency food from America's Second Harvest each year.

• Hungry Americans are primarily women, children, the elderly, and individuals who suffer from disabilities.

• One in every four people in a soup kitchen line is a child.

• Thirty-six percent of the recipients of food at a food bank have had to choose between buying food or paying for housing.

• Forty-five percent of the recipients of emergency food assistance have had to choose between buying food and paying for utilities or heat.

• Thirty percent of the recipients of food at a food bank have had to choose between buying food and paying for medical care or medicine.

• Severe and even mild under-nutrition can cause long-term harm to the cognitive, physical, social, and psychological development of a child.

• Nearly 39 percent of households receiving emergency food assistance have at least one working adult.

Hunger relief depends on volunteers and donations. Indeed, volunteers donate over $11 million in unpaid work every week at local hunger-relief agencies. The ratio of volunteers to paid staff in kitchen pantries is 8 to 1, and of volunteers to paid staff in soup kitchens, 16 to 3. Many volunteers are recruited through faith-based organizations and local hunger-relief charities. They are usually trained for their work as well as for their interaction with agency staff and recipients (O'Brien and Aldeen 2001). The hospitality community could join the volunteers by working in these and many other specific ways unique to our industry.

Determining how hospitality students could participate in service-learning experiences while developing professionally begins with an examination of the hospitality curriculum. A typical model of coursework for a two- or four-year hospitality degree generally includes: (1) foundation courses in general education, (2) required hospitality major courses, (3) additional required courses designed to enhance or support the major, such as computer and business courses, and (4) electives. Among the major courses one usually finds a significant study of food. Although hospitality programs vary in the number of required food-focused courses, no hospitality major graduates without studying foodservice. Students learn about foodservice in many ways: a hands-on, laboratory setting; required industry hours; an internship or cooperative experience; textbooks, guest speakers, career fairs, and trips to industry trade shows; and combinations of these experiences. Even in programs that allow a specialization in other aspects of the major, students cannot totally avoid exposure to foodservice, an area central to the hospitality field. An examination of the courses in hospitality programs typically reveals specific food-related courses such as Principles of Food Production, Nutrition, Food Sanitation and Safety, Quantity Foodservice Management, Foodservice Cost Control, and Purchasing. Culinary and two-year foodservice-only programs often have many more courses in food preparation and foodservice.

Upon graduation, hospitality majors leave college to work as restaurant managers, hotel managers, noncommercial foodservice operators, meeting planners, club managers; on cruise ships or at resorts; or for state tourism departments, destination-management organizations, and many other types of hospitality positions. Common to all of these is the need to plan, prepare, coordinate, and arrange meals for guests. Again, the connection with food is central. The type of community service activities begun during college through service-learning can be extended and expanded throughout an individual's career. Opportunities to support hunger-relief activities provide a seamless transition from college work to managerial settings.

Getting Started

Service-learning activities should be meaningful to both the students and the community. They also should be challenging, enlightening, rewarding, positive, empowering, and fun! Although "fun" may seem out of place, it necessarily becomes part of the experience when we speak about the hospitality industry and especially about hospitality majors.

All service-learning activities involve advance planning. Goals include assessing the needs of the community and the students, and balancing the challenges and available support and resources. The preliminary steps involve collaborating with a community representative to determine the needs and how students might be able to meet them in a meaningful learning activity. Resources, such as time and money, and logistics and the scope of the project should be agreed upon in advance (McCarthy 1996).

Introductory service-learning experiences often begin with a one-time, short-term activity (McCarthy 1996). The project needs to take into consideration the time students have available and the difficulty of the services they expect to provide. Important to this initial learning experience is success. This activity can be the foundation for interest and enthusiasm for future service-learning projects.

For hospitality majors, this might be a project such as preparing meals for special families at Thanksgiving. The service-learning goals would include providing the students with information that would help them learn more about the community setting of the university, as well as learning more about social issues that may be far removed from their own lives. This could involve research on the Internet about hunger and inviting a guest speaker from a local agency to describe the issues of hunger, homelessness, and unemployment in the community. This might also be an opportunity for an extra-credit report on the history and tradition of an earlier form of restaurant/tavern, the British pub, where food, clothing, furniture, and money were collected and given to neighbors in need. Students would sharpen their critical thinking skills when they realize that simple answers are not usually appropriate for complex social problems (Lisman 1998).

Additionally, students would be involved in teamwork, leadership, and delegation of responsibility while planning and implementing the project, and would learn more about food purchasing, storage, and preparation, as well as sanitation, foodservice, and nutrition.

The final activities would include an evaluation of the success of the project, specific to the management of the event and food preparation and service. It may also be appropriate to reflect on students' reactions to their experiences. This could take the form of small group discussions on how they felt before and after the project: What was most meaningful to them? What is the meaning of service to the community? Students should also have an opportunity to celebrate their involvement, immediately after the event or shortly after, depending on the type and timing of the project. Any photos taken during the activity should be posted and shared with the community agency, and could also be used in a college newsletter or sent to the university or local newspaper (McCarthy 1996).

Another approach is to integrate the service-learning activity into a course (Enos and Troppe 1996). The service-learning activity becomes part of the course, rather than merely an add-on. It should advance the objectives of the course and give students the opportunity to see the subject matter in a different context. An example would be working at a soup kitchen or at a Kid's Café (the nation's largest charitable meal service program for needy children). Hospitality faculty and students generally think of food as fun, family, entertainment, and sometimes, art. Our students typically go out into the world to work in restaurants, sports bars, hotels, country clubs, and the like. Working at a soup kitchen or at a Kid's Café presents food in a completely different venue, as relief from hunger. The contemplation of our basic need for food to satisfy genuine hunger as well as nutrition for the development of a child's body and brain becomes a sobering scenario. It holds the potential of helping students explore ways in which their profession relates to social problems in our communities, and could be combined with research on hunger, nutrition, and human physiology.

Other options for a service-learning experience include independent study or a fourth-credit, where the student designs a service-learning project for extra credit in a particular course. In both cases, the student takes responsibility for designing the experience through planning with the faculty member and the agency administrator. The faculty member must approve the plan. Generally, the student meets on a predetermined basis with the agency administrator and the faculty member. The student keeps a journal and completes assignments and submits them for grading in a timely manner. Evaluation and reflection are the same as with group service-learning projects. Individual service-learning projects usually follow group projects when students know more about the agency and its needs and want to commit to various aspects of the program (Enos and Troppe 1996).

There are many examples of hospitality projects that serve the needs of the community and help in the professional socialization of hospitality students. The following list is a sampling of activities that could be used in hospitality courses, as one-time, short-term projects, student organization projects, ongoing projects, cocurricular projects, annual activities, independent studies, and so forth. Potential logistical problems in implementing some of these projects would require careful selection and planning. It may be necessary to select projects near campus, or to couple first-year students with upper-class students who can provide transportation. Student teams can help coordinate these activities. Some activities require more faculty supervision than others, but all of them require advance planning, coordination, and evaluation. As you work with your local food bank, perishable-food rescue agency, or soup kitchen, you will discover many other unmet needs with great potential for mutual benefits.

Sample Service-Learning Activities:
- Cook, serve, and clean up at a soup kitchen.
- Develop and teach a unit on sanitation to soup-kitchen truck drivers or receiving-agency staff and volunteers.
- Teach kitchen safety to community groups.
- Teach nutrition to community groups.
- Solicit perishable food from restaurants, hotels, and other food-service operations for distribution.
- Sort and repackage food for distribution.
- Demonstrate the proper use and care of commercial food preparation equipment.
- Demonstrate the safe use and storage of kitchen chemicals.
- Prepare food at a Kid's Café during the summer.
- Cook for a Head Start Program, camp, or Special Olympics.
- Teach children and youth about food and principles of food preparation.
- Work with local Girl and Boy Scout troops who need cooking skills for after-school independence.
- Plan and prepare foods for special events for philanthropic organizations.
- Prepare food for Habitat for Humanity volunteers.
- Design and implement publicity campaigns for food banks, soup kitchens, etc.
- Develop recipes for unusual food donations.
- Help in a kitchen station at a Community Kitchen.
- Assist a chef at a Community Kitchen.
- Teach assigned units on food-related topics at a Community Kitchen.
- Work at Ronald McDonald House and other similar operations.
- Organize a university chapter of a hunger-relief organization.
- Organize a meeting with other on-campus student hunger coalitions, to network and coordinate volunteer activities.
- Research hunger issues locally, nationally, and internationally.
- Teach computer skills to agency employees and program participants.

Service-Learning in Practice

An example of a service-learning project for the Hotel, Restaurant & Institutional Management (HRIM) program at the University of Delaware began with a conversation between the CEO of the Food Bank of Delaware and a faculty member. Asked about how the HRIM program might be of help to the food bank, the CEO responded that what they needed *least* was a group collection of more cans of diced beets, which used little of the skills of hospitality students. What they did need was help with their annual meeting, which, for the first time, was to include a luncheon. Two planning sessions with other faculty led to a commitment to use the event as a project for the catering class. A junior student taking an independent study did additional planning and work on the event, and student teams were set up.

The event was to have a Southwest theme and be held in the warehouse at the food bank. The menu and even the centerpieces were designed using products from the food bank. The food was prepared at the HRIM laboratory kitchen with products delivered by a food-bank refrigerated truck. Student servers wore jeans, white shirts, white aprons, bandanas, and cowboy hats. On long tables, set up end-to-end and covered with white butcher paper, centerpieces were placed made from canned foods arranged on a bandana and topped with a live cactus. Country music CDs were donated by food-bank staff and played on a portable CD player positioned beside the microphone.

Smiling "hoe-down students" served the food, consisting of crois-sant sandwiches of chicken salad, coleslaw, dill potato salad, fruit salad, crudités, chips, a brownie, and a candy bar. Canned soft drinks, fruit punch, water, and coffee were also served. Frankly, it was not exactly Southwest cuisine, nor was it all nutritious, but no one seemed to notice.

The attendees were a diverse group of people, including partici-pants in food-bank programs, soup-kitchen staff from across the state, and other recipient agency staff, as well as representatives of faith-based groups, food-bank volunteers, and city and state political leaders. There were people dressed in business suits and people dressed casually. A few came with children and babies. The theme, music, students, menu, and location set the tone and helped bring a festive feeling to the gathering. It was a time to acknowledge and thank those who had helped the food bank over the past year, and celebrate new opportunities for the coming year. Congressman Mike Castle was the keynote speaker. Photos of the event were used by the press, the food bank, and the HRIM program.

The event helped students develop their skills in planning and executing an event, and reinforced their knowledge of food safety and sanitation, quantity food preparation, food storage, teamwork, delegation, and leadership. In addition they learned about the work of a food bank and discovered the immensity of the operation. They met and joked with the staff of the food bank while setting up for the event. They helped turn a big warehouse into a setting for a banquet with a theme, music, a few decorations, and a lot of hospitality. Many of them shook hands with Congressman Castle and learned more about the community. The students have not forgotten this experience, and the people at the food bank have not forgotten them.

This event was a positive experience for the Food Bank of Delaware, our students, the HRIM program, and the University of Delaware. Because of this initial step, the relationship has grown and we have formed a growing partnership with the agency. We have been involved with every annual meeting banquet since that first one.

It would be difficult to say whether we have adopted them or they have adopted us, but we have worked together in several different ways. When they began their produce program, one of our faculty members taught sanitation to their drivers and recipient agencies, something that could have been done by students in a training course, an HR course, as a project for Eta Sigma Delta, or as an independent study. When they held a fundraising "50s party" at a local Embassy Suites, our students sold raffle tickets and served food while decked out like the cast of "Grease," with ducktails and ponytails and wearing saddle oxfords and tee-shirts with packages of cigarettes rolled up in the sleeves. Our program bonded even more firmly when a faculty member who is an architect designed their community kitchen, an activity that is beyond the capability of an HRIM undergraduate. This faculty member has also served as an excellent role model for our students by offering his talents.

As this relationship evolved and we repeatedly remarked on the importance of service-learning, we decided to make a major commitment to service-learning, which has greater potential now than ever in the past. The Food Bank of Delaware has been funded for a community kitchen, which is a foodservice training program where people are taught practical culinary skills, food sanitation, teamwork, and life skills training. These programs are often located in food banks or in perishable-food rescue operations where food has been donated by restaurants, hotels, hospitals, noncommercial foodservice operations, caterers, and the like. The trainees at these programs usually have little or no hospitality job training but want to begin working in the hospitality field. The premier program of this type is the DC Central Kitchen, where trainees prepare food for the homeless using donated rescued food. They cook with purchased foods for catered events in their Fresh Start Catering operation, and have also opened a Fresh Start Bakery which has contracted to bake for local hotels and special events. Incidentally, more than 7,000 volunteers have worked at the DC Central Kitchen, from all across the world. This exemplary program has been the topic of "Nightline," and its former director, Robert Egger, has been honored on "Oprah." The staff is ready to assist any food bank or other group with startup activities and continuing help for initiating a community kitchen (www.dccentralkitchen.org). Robert Egger is aware of our potential to make a difference and is eager to see hospitality-management education join in the fight against hunger through service-learning activities.

As the community kitchen in Delaware evolves, there will be a much bigger role for the HRIM program. Students will be able to participate in the solicitation of donated foods from restaurants, hotels, noncommercial foodservice operations, hospitals, and others. They will also be able to help train foodservice workers and assist in the kitchen; develop standardized quantity recipes from food-bank products; train volunteers; and possibly branch out and work in soup kitchens or one of many other hunger agencies, helping with sanitation and proper use of donated foods. We expect to see our partnership with the Food Bank of Delaware expand as we further commit to service-learning.

The Immersion Plan

We are in the process of what might be called a total immersion plan. Having changed our mission statement to include service-learning as a primary educational goal, we require our students to work 800 hours in the industry before graduation, and have adjusted a portion of that time to include 100 volunteer hours in a community setting of their choice. Additionally, we will be granting scholarships for students who distinguish themselves with hospitality service-learning activities.

We are setting the stage for service-learning, beginning with our Introduction to Hospitality course, which includes a tour of the Food Bank of Delaware. Students view a videotape on hunger, receive pamphlets with the latest statistics on hunger, and conduct Internet research on hunger and poverty topics. Throughout their matriculation, they will be involved in other co-curricular projects, and by the time they graduate they will be very familiar with the subject of hunger, the Food Bank of Delaware, perishable food rescue, the community kitchen, and the Kid's Café. They will have established traditions and memories in volunteer activities that they can continue in their work settings.

Now More Than Ever

In their recent research, Eyler and Giles (1999) found that students developed greater tolerance for others, and appreciated other cultures more, as a result of their experiences in service-learning. Students said they felt that others were more like them than they expected and that their experience resulted in fewer negative stereotypes. They also believed that they understood themselves better, felt better about themselves, and experienced a growing sense of personal competence after participating in service-learning. These are all positive experiences that will better enable students to meet the diverse issues of the future.

Service-learning is important for the hospitality program because it provides positive recognition for the community and the university. Additionally, it facilitates a relationship between students and other volunteers, including restaurateurs, wholesale food distributors and food manufacturers, local and state political leaders, other community leaders, and program participants. For the same reasons, hospitality faculty benefit personally from being an active part of the community. Furthermore, as community volunteers, faculty leave lasting impressions as role models for students.

In his book *Learned Optimism*, Martin Seligman describes the alarming increase of depression among young people in our culture, which he convincingly attributes to excessive focus on the individual and "a diminished sense of community and loss of higher purpose" (1998: 284). A part of the cure he recommends is investing ourselves in our communities and finding greater meaning in our lives. Service-learning is important for the individual because it provides students with opportunities to connect with the world in a larger sense, and move out of the insular context of the college campus. It gives them a connection that makes them feel good about themselves.

Following the events of September 11, nearly every magazine and television psychologist's commentary suggested that moving out into our communities and volunteering would greatly facilitate overcoming grief and fear. As shown by the examples in this essay, there are many reasons to join the service-learning movement. We have sufficient faculty and students to truly make a difference. Succinctly stated:

• We have a worthwhile cause in a country that needs active citizens.

• We have expertise to share.

• We have students and faculty who will benefit both professionally and personally.

Now is the time.

References

Bok, Derek. (1982). *Beyond the Ivory Tower: Social Responsibilities of the Modern University.* Cambridge, MA: Harvard University Press.

Boyer, Ernest L. (1988). *College: The Undergraduate Experience in America.* New York: Harper & Row.

_____. (1990). *Scholarship Reconsidered: Priorities for the Professoriate.* Lawrenceville, NJ: Princeton University Press.

Cameron, Mark, Ann Forsyth, William A. Green, Henry Lu, Patricia McGirr, Patsy Eubanks Owens, and Ronald Stoltz. (2001). "Learning through Service: The Community Design Studio." *College Teaching* 49 (3):105-113.

Checkoway, Barry. (2001). "Renewing the Civic Mission of the American Research University." *Journal of Higher Education* 72 (2):125-148.

Commission for Educational Quality. (1985). *Access to Quality Undergraduate Education.* Atlanta, GA: Southern Region Education Board.

Dewey, John. (1938). *Experience and Education.* New York: Macmillan Publishing Company, Inc.

Enos, Sandra L., and Marie L.Troppe. (1996). "Service-Learning in the Curriculum." In *Service-Learning in Higher Education.* Edited by B. Jacoby et al., 156-181. San Francisco, CA: Jossey-Bass, Inc.

Eyler, Janet, and Dwight E. Giles, Jr. (1999). *Where's the Learning in Service-Learning?* San Francisco, CA: Jossey-Bass, Inc.

Howard, Jeffrey. (2000-2001). "Academic Service-Learning: Myths, Challenges, and Recommendations," *Teaching Excellence — Toward the Best in the Academy* 12 (3):1-2.

_____. (1996). "Service-Learning in Today's Higher Education." In *Service-Learning in Higher Education.* Edited by B. Jacoby et al., 3-22. San Francisco, CA: Jossey-Bass, Inc.

Jacoby, B., et al. (1996). *Service-Learning in Higher Education: Concepts and Practices.* San Francisco, CA: Jossey-Bass.

Kezar, Adrianna, and Robert A. Rhoads. (March 2001). "The Dynamic Tensions of Service-Learning in Higher Education." *Journal of Higher Education* 72 (2):148-166.

Lisman, David C. (1998). *Toward a Civil Society — Civic Literacy and Service-Learning.* Westport, CT: Bergin & Garvey.

Loschert, Kristen. (August 2001). "In the Service of Learning or Just Learning to Serve?" *Community College Week* 13 (26): 6.

Lucas, Christopher J. (1994). *American Higher Education: A History*. New York: St. Martin's Griffin.

McCarthy, Mark D. (1996). "One-Time and Short-Term Service-Learning Experiences." In *Service-Learning in Higher Education*. Edited by B. Jacoby et al., 113-134. San Francisco, CA: Jossey-Bass, Inc.

O'Brien, Doug, and Halley Torres Aldeen. (2001). *Hunger in America 2001. Third National Hunger Study*. Chicago, IL: America's Second Harvest.

Rice, R. Eugene. (1996). *Making a Place for the New American Scholar*. Washington, DC: American Association for Higher Education.

Seligman, Martin E. P. (1998). *Learned Optimism*. New York: Alfred A. Knopf, Inc.

Assessing the Personal Impact of a Service-Learning Course Based in a Hospitality-Management Program at Cornell University

by Therese A. O'Connor, Marge Dill, Nancy Burston, and Stephanie Rainsford

Service-Learning and Community Partnerships

Many college academic programs, especially those like hotel management and social work that are service-oriented, have historically included experiential learning. But they have rarely included a true service-learning curriculum, defined by Stanton (1987) and others as an approach to experiential learning and an expression of values including community development and empowerment, social and educational exchange, and, very importantly, reciprocal learning. Scholars have identified the ideal goals of American education as including respect, caring, trust, and cooperation, reflected in a curriculum and a pedagogy that promote democracy and conscious citizenship (Seigel and Rockwood 1993). Experiential education coupled with well-designed service-learning components could include and reinforce these ideals.

Only recently have college administrators and faculty begun to embrace the notion of service-learning partnerships developed and sustained through the curriculum. Holland and Gelmon (1998) attribute the traditional failure of universities in community partnerships to an inability to look beyond their own self-interest, causing them to create one-sided approaches to school-community links. This limited view has prevented universities from cultivating an array of partnerships capable of sustaining a strong connection with the community. Universities have not typically put in place the ideals of democratically based education and social responsibility as expressed by Dewey (1916) and others.

If an institution of higher education cannot sustain good community partnerships and programs, it becomes even more difficult for students at that institution to embrace the importance of having a connection to their community. The ideas of social and civic responsibility and democratically based education become academic lip service, and community partnership, except as a self-serving exercise, remains a foreign concept in many academic realms.

In "Death of a Dream," Don Hill (1998) claims that service-learning has suffered from a self-delusion: "Service-learning programs began as partnerships seeking to connect organizations that were previously separate. Few, however, went much beyond being partners in name and money" (30). This has certainly been true of many education-community collaborative efforts as well as partnerships between for-profits and not-for-profits.

Service-learning, which has been increasingly incorporated into curricula, has historically had an orientation toward charitable, not-for-profit enterprises and programs. Students have usually worked in public school districts, community centers, libraries, museums, and social-service agencies. Often students have been involved in trying to obtain donations, grants, and gifts-in-kind from for-profit companies, but they have not been closely tied to any kind of long-term partnership, nor have they helped to forge such a partnership between community entities.

Moreover, students have not been particularly involved in the creation or maintenance of partnerships between for-profits and not-for-profits. Is it possible to offer students the possibility of being involved in creating these partnerships? Do students have enough savvy? Do they understand the implications of attempting to forge these complex partnerships? What would it take to involve students in a three-way partnership involving not-for-profit programs, for-profit partners, and academic interests? In the face of a lukewarm commitment to community service by many universities, how can we ask students to become involved in partnerships? Or, to put the question another way, do we enlist students into the status quo of service-learning or do we encourage them to attempt to affect change in the relationship among such powerful entities as higher education, business, and the community in which they reside? These are some of the questions we explore in this paper by reviewing a university service-learning course and student perspectives, and by exploring community perspectives and designs for potential projects.

The Housing and Feeding the Homeless Course: A Review

The Housing and Feeding the Homeless course at Cornell University was created in 1987 as a result of the president's initiative for integrating and improving undergraduate education. An important consideration was to bring together the areas of business, specifically hospitality business, and human/social services by creating a vehicle whereby the students in those two disciplines could apply their classroom learning while exploring issues and concerns of the local community. This also represented an attempt to create a partnership between two heretofore unconnected fields of study, and was considered a truly innovative educational program.

Over the years, more than 500 students have gained incredible insight and have had enriching experiences through their community work associated with the course. They have worked with not-for-profit social-service and human service agencies, and have produced meaningful and useful products for various groups (see box). Yet, we wonder if they have grasped the real potential of collaboration between the for-profit and not-for-profit worlds; whether they have asked if a corporate or business social conscience exists, or who, if anyone, is responsible for tending to the ills of a community's disenfranchised members. Surely such questions are relevant to the concept of democratically based education.

Examples of Service-Learning Projects Completed by Students Since 1994

- Telethon on local access television that raised over $5,000: Loaves & Fishes community soup kitchen

- Film for training volunteers to work in shelters: American Red Cross, Tompkins County

- Meal voucher program for runaway youth: Hillside Bridges for Youth Program

- Database organization and development for donors and grants agencies: Loaves & Fishes community soup kitchen

- Development and production of monthly newsletter for residents: McCormick Detention Center, NYS Division for Youth

- Client database development for Emergency Services Division: Tompkins County Department of Social Services

- Development of health curriculum for very young children: Tompkins County Head Start Program

- Feasibility study for a Prepared and Perishable Food Rescue Program: Ithaca-area hotels, restaurants, and colleges

---

Service-learning has historically rested on various rationales that have included youth development, prevention of the development of "troubled" or disenfranchised youth, social and civic responsibility issues, the relevance of academic learning, and the relationship of service-learning to career options (Bhaerman and Gomez 1998: 11). In the Housing and Feeding the Homeless course, we have attempted to focus primarily on the civic and social responsibility aspects by combining lectures, readings, and discussion with what we call personal contact community service work.

We assume that when college students work directly with community agencies and their clients, they gain a better understanding of the effects of public policy and government programs at the personal level. They begin to understand the concepts of social responsibility, democratically based education, and community partnerships. Since the course's inception, students have worked in homeless shelters, community soup kitchens and other meal programs, equal-opportunity corporations, Head Start centers, subsidized housing projects, urban 4-H programs, juvenile detention centers, and youth respite programs. They have worked face-to-face with clients and families as well as with agency managers.

The course hosts six to seven speakers each semester from both the private and the public sectors, from for-profit and not-for-profit enterprises. The idea of partnerships is discussed at length, including examples of many programs around the country. Speakers come from real estate and low-income housing development, job training programs, banking, urban shelter programs, urban and rural youth programs, food banks, city and regional planning, hospitality companies involved in partner programs, and citizen advocacy groups. By the end of the semester, students have fulfilled a minimum of 25 hours of community service work. Some students, while earning four credits, have completed approximately 64 hours of work involving a special project.

In the course we have attempted to explore, but not to create, partnerships between social service agencies and businesses within the community. The students, through service-learning, have worked almost exclusively with one side of this potential partnership: the not-for-profit side. Our focus here, then, centers on student knowledge of and attitudes toward social service-business collaborations, and how we might design service-learning projects that include a three-way experience among students, human service agencies, and for-profit businesses.

Course Survey and Responses

We have endeavored to explore student attitudes about their service work through a post-semester survey that has been used in the course since 1996. Students have also used logs and journals to record and reflect upon their community experiences. What follows focuses on the survey responses as a way to envision potential community-academic partnerships.

The survey attempts to evaluate (1) knowledge of for-profit and not-for-profit solutions to homelessness and hunger, (2) knowledge of partnerships in community work, and (3) perceptions of which industries or businesses can best address poverty, homelessness, and hunger. The survey explores attitudes in two realms: personal and career-oriented questions link attitudes about poverty and homelessless to personal values and career choices; and a second group of questions, outlined below in the Attachment, identifies attitudes about social responsibility and community partnerships. The 10 questions highlighted in this chapter ask students whether they believe particular industries or businesses can address issues of poverty, homelessness, or hunger. They also attempt to determine whether students have any knowledge of potential community partnerships that could address these problems.

The survey, designed by former Cornell students Aileen Huang and Jennifer Schwartz in collaboration with the course instructor, was first tested for clarity by 10 students and faculty not associated with the course. It is distributed at the end of each semester during which topics related to community development and partnerships (among others) have been discussed at length. Of 76 surveys distributed, there have been 40 responses, a return rate of 53 percent. Responses are calibrated to a basic five-point Likert-type scale with the "unknown/neutral" response put at 5 in an attempt to discourage the typical central, neutral response. Responses are worded: 1 = strongly disagree, 2 = disagree, 3 = agree, 4 = strongly agree, 5 = don't know. Every question on the 40 returned surveys had a response.

Responses were totaled for each question and converted to percentages. For this chapter, simple totals for the whole sample were reviewed. Although an analysis by school affiliation sub-group (e.g., hotel students compared to arts and sciences students) might prove interesting, the small sample size limits its value.

The results of the 10 questions highlighted here do not point to astounding conclusions. In fact, most attitude and opinion surveys prove inconclusive. However, based on some of the responses obtained, we may be able to focus educational energy and service-learning programming on what students feel they do or do not know about community partnerships.

The first significant response is that an overwhelming majority of this sample, 80 percent, felt that American business has a responsibility to its community in addressing poverty and hunger. Of course, there was a bias here, in that respondents voluntarily enrolled in this course and presumably had an interest in community and social responsibility. An open-ended question on the survey (question 21) corroborated this result.

It is clear from the responses that the students were unsure what industries might be most effective in addressing poverty and homelessness. Approximately 42 percent of the responses to industry-related questions were "Don't know." In a related manner, 43 percent were unsure whether the public or private sectors offered better solutions to poverty and homelessness.

One of the most interesting findings is that 61 percent of the students felt they did not have a good understanding of public-private partnerships. This is disappointing, considering the fact that a good amount of information and guest-speaker and lecture time are devoted to the topic. However, 50 percent of the respondents felt they did understand how public and private organizations separately address the issues of homelessness and hunger. These two results may point to a flaw in the method of presenting the concept of community partnerships, or they may suggest that the concept is difficult to grasp because of its complexity. (Consider, for example, the many elements that constitute a government-subsidized for-profit initiative such as Marriott International's Pathways Program.)

It would appear that we have a student audience that is ripe to challenge the status quo if we as educators are able to give it tools. The potential for exploring partnerships through first-hand community service work is exciting.

A Student Perspective

Students need to overcome two obstacles to explore three-way partnerships (student/for-profit/not-for-profit). One is their lack of knowledge of the funding strategies in these two realms and how they might interface. The other is lack of knowledge about the structure and goals of two very different organizational types. However, students, particularly students in hospitality or business programs, can still offer not-for-profit businesses much in the way of expertise.

Students working with not-for-profit organizations have discovered, through service-learning courses, that for-profit organizations have funds available for not-for-profit organizations and are willing to work with them. Businesses reserve these funds for "charitable organizations," and while the types of charitable organizations that qualify may be restricted, the funds are clearly available if the appropriate requirements are fulfilled. Not-for-profit organizations often ask for donations or volunteers for a specific project or an annual or one-time event. This arrangement has its benefits: the not-for-profit organizations welcome the donations, while businesses gain positive public relations as well as tax write-offs. Since the not-for-profit organizations continue to work on their own, businesses do not have to commit time or other nonmonetary resources. This kind of arrangement creates little demand on either type of organization to set up permanent partnerships.

The concept of community partnerships — that is, two or more organizations (for-profit and not-for-profit) defining goals, committing resources, and working together — is fairly easy to understand in theory, but most students are not exposed to partnerships of this kind. Lack of familiarity with programs such as STRIVE or Marriott's Pathways program makes it difficult for students to think of specific community partnership models. Students who have been exposed to partnerships like these do not necessarily understand how they work and what benefits each partner receives.

Students need to understand the complexity of each component of the partnership in order to develop a three-way partnership model. One possibility would be to create a permanent student internship in which each student worked with both for-profit and not-for-profit organizations. The student's goal would be to maintain a partnership between the two organizations. Such a permanent internship would establish long-term continuity by ensuring that there would always be at least one student attempting to maintain the relationship. The student could work with for-profit and not-for-profit organizations to develop "best fit" arrangements that help both organizations benefit from their alliance and achieve their goals.

Many university programs, including that of the School of Hotel Administration at Cornell University, sponsor business internship programs to enhance students' work experiences. Many students work for large companies such as Marriott, Hilton, Aramark, and the Myriad Restaurant Group. While working for these companies, they gain valuable experience they can bring back to the classroom and eventually use in their careers, but this knowledge does not need to stay in the classroom or be used only for personal advantage. It can benefit not-for-profit organizations as well. Developing a program to link student work experiences in for-profit businesses and not-for-profit businesses may be beneficial for students, for-profit businesses, and not-for-profit organizations at the same time.

An example might work as follows. The surplus food donated to soup kitchens can sometimes be overwhelming. Often, ingredients are donated that amateur chefs or cooks do not know how to use, so they tend to sit in storage until they spoil and are thrown away. Students studying hospitality, agriculture, nutrition, and culinary arts learn how to prepare these ingredients as well how to assess their nutritional value. The Contemporary Healthy Foods course offered in the Hotel School enrolls students studying restaurant operations, independent agriculture, and nutrition. It teaches them about healthful foods, their nutritional value, and how to use them in various dishes. The students visit organic farms and work with local chefs to produce a dinner event that features local products in healthy dishes.

The purpose of this event is to enable the farmers and restaurants to network and develop a beneficial relationship. During the semester, the students work to develop these networks, but they might also be able to encourage relationships among farmers, restaurants, and not-for-profit organizations. For example, the chefs and farmers teach amateur soup-kitchen cooks how to prepare dishes with donated ingredients; several not-for-profit organizations offer nutrition classes, which would be enhanced by the farmers' knowledge and experience; and the students arrange for the restaurant chef to be a guest chef or trainer at the soup kitchen for an evening or afternoon.

What benefits would accrue to the different partners? Farmers would receive free marketing within the community. Restaurateurs would receive publicity and positive public relations — free advertising. Soup kitchens would learn how to use ingredients that might otherwise have to be discarded, besides receiving a food donation and improving their nutritional knowledge.

Another example might be in the area of business-control systems. Students studying hospitality learn about control systems in introductory food and beverage management courses as well as in their accounting and finance courses. There is also an upper-level class in the Hotel School, entitled Internal Control, in which students work with a local business to survey and analyze the organization's internal control system. Although these students learn a great deal about internal controls and what practices are more effective than others, they never develop and implement their own self-designed control system with a company or business. However, if they were able to develop a partnership between a business and a not-for-profit organization, they could use the classroom material to survey and analyze the local business, and then develop and implement an inventory control system for a not-for-profit organization. The business could act as a sponsor or mentor for the not-for-profit, with the student acting as a liaison person or facilitator.

Principles of Collaboration

The not-for-profit community of Tompkins County relies heavily on the contributions of volunteers from the community at large and, in particular, on the time and energy provided by members of the academy. This relationship, traditionally a two-way partnership between agencies and students and faculty, could be broadened into a three-way partnership that includes the for-profit community. Many basic principles of partnering would still apply. First, as in any collaboration, all parties must perceive a benefit that outweighs any negative side effects. The points discussed below are essential if a collaboration is to succeed.

Choice. Students should be able to choose from an array of potential projects to ensure that both the for-profit and not-for-profit organizations view the activity as a priority and can commit staff time to it. Even if the students have developed an excellent proposal, the project will not succeed unless the other entities support it. In addition, if the focus of the project is not consistent with the goals of the partner organizations, the students are unlikely to get the assistance they need to accomplish their service-learning goals. There is nothing worse for busy staff than being unconvinced of the value of a project and spending time helping students who only think they are helping an organization.

Timing. Just as faculty and students have time constraints, so do for-profit and not-for-profit organizations. Each entity needs to learn about the other and be flexible. Many projects extend well beyond the length of a typical semester, may not be completed in 12 or 14 weeks, or may need follow-up.

Job/Project Description. Before a match can be made, there needs to be a clear written understanding of what the project hopes to accomplish. The for-profit and not-for-profit entities should attempt to outline the learning skills they think the student can and should acquire, in order to emphasize that the project is understood as a service-learning.

Matching/Screening Process. The mechanics for finding a good project match remain the same, even with the addition of other partners. Once the for-profit and not-for-profit entities have spelled out precisely their needs and requirements, the student must be matched with an appropriate project. As in a job search, the student contacts an organization by telephone, letter, or email to request an interview, and follows up the initial contact with a resume. A brief telephone interview is often useful for initial screening purposes, covering topics such as general interests, basic technical skills, time availability, and transportation issues. For example, if a student lacks expertise with a computer program that is required, it would be a waste of everyone's time to proceed. Likewise, if some of the work needs to be carried out on weekday mornings, and the student's schedule includes classes every morning, the match cannot be successful, even with everyone's good intentions. If routine items like these cannot be easily resolved, the student should be redirected to other organizations.

A face-to-face interview is essential following telephone contact. This is when the interested parties need to assess the student's skills and interests in relation to the details of the potential project. A student who expects to gain direct experience with clients through a project that is primarily administrative represents a mismatch. Technical skills are somewhat easier to evaluate than attributes such as motivation, resourcefulness, reliability, flexibility, and creativity, but, depending on the type of project proposed, particular attributes may need to be evaluated.

Working Expectations. Some projects require more independent work on the part of the students than others. This should be specified up front, so that misunderstandings can be avoided. However, in all projects, the students need oversight, supervision, monitoring, feedback, recognition, and support from the not-for-profit and for-profit partners. This takes time, planning, and follow-through. The agency and business staff need to recognize and convey to the students how their work would fit into the bigger picture — how the student contribution could make a real difference.

Clearinghouse. The Human Services Coalition (HSC) acts as an informal clearinghouse for helping students and not-for-profit organizations match their needs. "The Guide to Volunteer Opportunities in Tompkins County," an information and referral service publication compiled with assistance from students at the Cornell University Public Service Center, is useful to both students and agencies looking for appropriate resources. Could an agency like HSC act as a clearinghouse to connect for-profit/not-for-profit projects with members of the academic community? This is an interesting possibility but would need serious commitment from each party.

Potential Models for Three-Way Partnerships

Here are some hypothetical scenarios or potential service-learning projects that could involve students in an organized learning situation with a for-profit business, and that could also benefit a for-profit business, advance the students' education, and strengthen the community:

Grocery Stores and Restaurants. These enterprises are already involved in gleaning operations with soup kitchens and food pantries, but more efficiency could be gained, thereby serving more community residents. (In Tompkins County, the number of free meal recipients is growing for the second year in a row, and although no one is turned away, the amount and nutritional content of the meals are sometimes less than desirable.) Moreover, according to *Hunger: The Faces and Facts,* published by America's Second Harvest (1998), there is a movement away from canned foods and toward fresh and frozen food. Although this trend is presumably good — driven by changes in the diet of the nation's population — it does present a challenge to food pantries and grocery stores. Timing of a pickup, use, and storage are the most obvious challenges. Students could be involved creating a sustainable partnership between two entities: for example, a major supermarket and two community meal programs.

In a partnership, the grocery store would not only gain community goodwill and public relations but would reduce or contain the costs of solid waste disposal — a serious problem in this time of higher fees for municipal services. The not-for-profits would gain by being able to meet the increasing need for their services. Local government could slow the rate of funding increases for food and, over time, reduce the public cost of waste management.

The challenge of working in both the for-profit and the not-for-profit worlds would give students a knowledge of solid waste management and teach them about the nutritional needs of recipients of emergency food systems. They could also help organize communications systems, analyze the pros and cons of different ways of doing business, and explore cost containment. Finally, they could hone skills in writing and rhetoric needed to write a grant for additional equipment such as freezers or coolers.

Developmental and Environmental Impact. An environmental impact statement is usually required whenever a major development project like a hotel or airport is proposed. There would seem to be more challenges now than ever before to new proposals. Although a proposal may be "good" in providing more jobs, it may not sit well with communities adjacent to the new facility. The discussion usually involves government agencies and private financing corporations, for-profit development and construction companies, and community residents. Residents may themselves be divided over the question of whether the jobs gained are worth the expense of disrupting the community.

National Public Radio recently aired a report about an airport in Kentucky that was going to expand significantly. More jobs would be created, since the airport would become a hub for UPS or a similar freight and air express business. However, air traffic and noise would also increase enormously, and the project would require relocation of a nearby blue collar community.

Initially, the development company's proposal was to bulldoze houses in the way and pay the expense of relocating families to new homes. But the residents objected that this would not address their concerns about the neighborhood or the community. Hence, the development company agreed to build a "new neighborhood" and move the entire community about five to 10 miles farther into the country. Now the rural folks, who were used to looking out their windows at fields and hills and encountering little traffic, were concerned. They objected to this new proposal, and one contingent of the opposition even suggested that a wall be put around the new community. Concern with "class differences" or "life-style differences" also came into play.

Clearly, the situation was fraught with learning opportunities, and students from fields like hotel development, architecture, engineering, and city planning, to name just a few, could play some kind of role. The for-profit companies, whether development or construction businesses, as well as the airlines and transport haulers would all benefit from a more rapid solution to their problem, and students assigned the task of working with any of these entities could help improve communication and expedite decision making. They would learn about community planning, home design and housing development, the law and regulations pertaining to environmental impact statements, and private and governmental financing possibilities.

In the end, the communities would obtain a better project with less environmental impact and personal disruption.

Transportation — Service Enhancement. This learning experience would link two different government offices and a for-profit company. Students could be based with any of these entities or with a not-for-profit agency that would also be involved.

Transportation is one of the barriers that must be overcome if welfare reform initiatives are to succeed. As anyone who has tried to get people to carpool or to use alternative travel knows, transportation issues are especially difficult. Hence, an outside stimulus — such as a student project — could be very useful. In Tompkins County, the coordinated public transportation system, Tompkins County Area Transit (TCAT), is progressive in its services. One of them, for example, called demand response, enables a bus on a regular route to be diverted to pick up a particular customer.

For a service-learning project, students could facilitate the coordination between the public transportation system and a major employer or several mid-size employers in an industrial technology park or professional center. With the assistance of the Department of Social Services or one of its contract agencies, students could identify job-eligible clients for whom transportation is a particular difficulty. Some public money is available to help with the costs incurred by potential employees, and public "incentive" money also exists for businesses that hire former welfare recipients.

Here is a situation where businesses can collaborate with public transportation companies to form a sustained partnership devoted to getting public-assistance recipients to work. By collaborating with the public transportation system, the businesses would not have to acquire vehicles of their own. Students could be involved in researching and designing transportation routes to accommodate the new employees, and might even suggest time and regional limits, company commitments, and other logistical and service details. Once the collaboration had been established, the public transportation system could also work with the Chamber of Commerce and other business organizations to promote the program.

In a project like this, students would learn about public transportation and develop the skills needed to work with employees and employers. They would sharpen their problem-solving and analytical skills in studying and projecting turnover rates, training costs, and the value of public dollars saved over time. The company, for its part, would have lower training and recruitment costs, because of higher rates of employee retention, and might eventually see reduced public-assistance spending by government or, perhaps more realistically, a slowing of the increase in such spending.

Human Resource Project — Job Retention. All workers face challenges in their daily lives, not just workers who have received public assistance. Some of the common but serious problems workers face include money management, alcohol and substance abuse, and health care. For several reasons, many companies have become more aware of and interested in educating their employees about personal health care issues.

Students in this scenario could attempt to link not-for-profit agencies that have expertise in personal health care areas to for-profit businesses interested in educating their staff about these issues. Students could work with not-for-profit agencies, while human resource staff at large companies, collaborating with the students, could identify issues they think their employees might want or need to learn more about. Information sessions or classes could be designed and orchestrated collaboratively by the students and the not-for-profit agencies. They could be offered at lunch or other convenient times during the work day. In recent years, especially in the area of health, industry has come to believe in prevention as a good investment. The proposed sessions would probably be viewed in the same way.

Students using surveying techniques in such a project would gain knowledge of the community's educational resources, improve their communication skills, and develop marketing strategies and techniques. The businesses, over time, might experience less absenteeism or increased employee retention, as well as have more focused and loyal employees. The community as a whole would gain a healthier, more informed, and perhaps less costly (in health care expense) work force.

Conclusion

Many important factors must be addressed when thinking and writing about potential three-way partnerships in a service-learning context. Most importantly, perhaps, all parties who might be involved must believe that the creation and sustainability of community partnerships is a valuable and worthwhile endeavor that will benefit all participants. Indeed, all participating parties would have to have substantive input into the design and evaluation of any program.

These kinds of hands-on, active community projects are complex at several levels. Students and faculty must understand the cultures, values, and philosophies of the for-profit and not-for profit organizations involved, and also be able to address the needs of both entities. Both kinds of organizations must be clear about what they want to accomplish and be willing to devote the time and energy needed for success.

Students must realize the importance of service-learning projects as "real" undertakings, and commit to seeing them through. They must also attempt to gain as much knowledge as possible about for-profit/not-for-profit partnerships and programs to use as a knowledge base for their service-learning experiences. For-profit and not-for-profit organizations must each be willing to allow them to learn, and must give them the responsibility and the authority to undertake meaningful tasks

Perhaps one of the biggest hurdles is the fact that most significant and valuable service-learning projects take longer than a typical semester's time. Faculty and administrators must be prepared to redesign curricula to allow service-learning courses to continue over two or three semesters, so that students can engage in worthwhile projects and achieve important goals. Only in this way will it be possible to break out of the service-learning model we have been using and begin to create new, complex partnerships.

Attachment. Selected Survey Questions and Responses

Sample = 40

2. I feel I have a good understanding of private-public partnerships that address issues of homelessness and hunger.
Strongly agree/Agree	32%
Strongly disagree/Disagree	61%
Don't know	5%

6. I have very little understanding of how public or private enterprises might address the concerns of hunger or homelessness.
Strongly agree/Agree	40%
Strongly disagree/Disagree	50%
Don't know	10%

11. I believe that private sector (both for-profit and non-profit) solutions to problems of homelessness and hunger have the best answers.
Strongly agree/Agree	25%
Strongly disagree/Disagree	30%
Don't know	45%

12. I believe that public sector solutions to homelessness and hunger have the best answers.
Strongly agree/Agree	15%
Strongly disagree/Disagree	45%
Don't know	40%

14. Because of its operational expertise, the hospitality industry can provide many solutions to the issues of homelessness and hunger.
Strongly agree/Agree	70%
Strongly disagree/Disagree	10%
Don't know	20%

17. I believe American businesses are obligated to address social problems of our society that include poverty, hunger, or homelessness.
Strongly agree/Agree	80%
Strongly disagree/Disagree	13%
Don't know	8%

18. The banking industry is the best industry for adequately addressing the problems of homelessness and hunger.
Strongly agree/Agree	0%
Strongly disagree/Disagree	55%
Don't know	45%

19. The social services/social work industry is the best industry for adequately addressing the problems of homelessness and hunger.

Strongly agree/Agree	38%
Strongly disagree/Disagree	30%
Don't know	33%

20. The hospitality industry is the best industry for adequately addressing the problems of homelessness and hunger.

Strongly agree/Agree	8%
Strongly disagree/Disagree	45%
Don't know	48%

21. Which industry(ies), if any, do you feel is/are the best one(s) for providing solutions to the problems of poverty, hunger, or homelessness? Please name/describe.

Response	Frequency*
All industries/business	15
No answer/don't know	13
Social services	6
Government	3
Hospitality industry	3
Church	2
Media	1
Advocacy groups	1

*These total more than the sample because some respondents listed more than one industry.

References

America's Second Harvest. (1998). *Hunger: The Faces and Facts.* Chicago: Second Harvest.

Bhaerman, R., K. Cordell, and B. Gomez. (1998). *The Role of Service-Learning in Educational Reform.* Raleigh, NC: National Society for Experiential Education.

Dewey, John. (1916). *Democracy and Education: An Introduction to the Philosophy of Education.* New York: MacMillan.

Hill, D. (1998). "Death of a Dream. Service-Learning 1994-2010: A Historical Analysis by One of the Dreamers." *NSEE Quarterly* 24 (1): 1-30.

Holland, Barbara, and Sherril Gelmon. (1998). "The State of the 'Engaged Campus.'" *American Association for Higher Education Bulletin* 51 (2): 3-6.

Seigel, S., and V. Rockwood. (1993). "Democratic Education, Student Empowerment, and Community Service: Theory and Practice." *Equity and Excellence in Education* 26 (2): 65-70.

Stanton, Timothy. (1987). "Service-Learning: Groping toward a Definition." *Experiential Education* 12 (1): 2-4.

Service-Learning Best Practices in Hospitality and Tourism Education

by Robert M. O'Halloran and Cynthia S. Deale

What do class projects, like a hotel-financial-management class conducting a feasibility study for a possible conference center, or a food-preparation class presenting a dinner for a local bishop or serving a seder dinner at a local synagogue, have to do with hospitality education? They are examples of service-learning opportunities that make learning more significant while encouraging students to participate in the community. They engage students in authentic experiences, enable them to use skills and knowledge learned in class, and are catalysts for much of the learning that takes place. Service-learning projects combine the most effective methods for improving self-efficacy, mastering experiences, and modeling (Tucker and McCarthy 2001).

The combination of service with learning has generated or renewed an abundance of related terms such as action research, civic literacy, collaborative learning, community-based education, community education, community service, cooperative education, cross cultural learning, education for social responsibility, experiential education, field study, internships, participatory research, public service, reciprocal learning, service-learning, servant leadership, social action, study service, volunteerism, and youth service. The language of service-learning has emerged because it best expresses the dialectic of meaningful community involvement with reflection (Hoyt and Thalman 2001).

Service-learning does not necessarily require new programs. It can also emerge from an examination of the compatibility of existing programs and courses with service-learning principles. The service-learning components of a program also provide an opportunity for the academy and the community to work together and enhance student and potential employee learning and leadership. There is no doubt that involving students fully in a learning experience increases learning, so hospitality educators need to find partnerships to facilitate learning in this field. Service-learning projects differ by clients, time commitment, and activities (Tucker, McCarthy, Hoxmeier, and Link 1998).

Service-learning partnerships, when effectively constructed and implemented, can emphasize quality and capitalize on the strengths of an industry and a community, while providing learners with:

- balance in the curriculum
- intellectual independence
- the ability to formulate problems
- the cultivation of new sensibilities
- affection for the subject matter
- critical thinking skills

The overall goal of the integration of these concepts is to broaden students' understanding of the needs of the community and the role industry can play in making any community a better place to live in and visit. The National Service-Learning Cooperative Clearinghouse has indicated that service-learning can have an effect on youth civic development. One hopes, therefore, that those students who are the future managers and leaders of the hospitality industry will carry such experiences, and the ethics and values they teach, with them wherever they may go.

This is especially important because there is perhaps no industry where controversial problems are more often found than in hospitality and tourism. Therefore, the integration of real projects into the curriculum with outcomes beneficial to the student and a community organization is a critical learning tool. In service-learning, students are often asked to take on problems or issues facing an organization or to provide a service for an organization. Students work through a definition of problems or issues, assess their complexity, identify the data or information needed to make a decision, and collect the data (analyzing, interpreting, and soliciting input from experts if necessary). They then participate in an authentic, rather than contrived, hands-on project that provides a service to the organization.

Service-Learning and Multiple Intelligences

Service-learning projects and exercises not only help develop thinking skills but are also useful in providing students with opportunities to use all of their intelligences. According to Howard Gardner (1983), who has developed the concept of multiple intelligences, the question to be asked is not "How smart is this person?" but "In what ways is this person smart?" (Donovan and Iovino 1997).

Gardner's idea is that there is no IQ, or measure of general intelligence. Instead, people have different ways of expressing their intelligence. Gardner has identified and described seven kinds of intelligence that people display to varying degrees: linguistic, logical-mathematical, musical, spatial, bodily-kinesthetic, interpersonal, and intrapersonal. Also, since he first identified these seven types, he has identified two more: naturalist intelligence and existentialist intelligence (Gardner 2003). Structuring a service-learning project or opportunity to take advantage of students' intelligences not only increases the learning opportunity but enables students to demonstrate their strengths and to work on areas that need improvement. For example, in the hospitality industry, chefs display spatial intelligence, especially when they are involved in presenting food. Students demonstrate and develop this type of intelligence when designing table arrangements. On the other hand, students planning to become managers need to develop their interpersonal intelligence, as indeed do all employees who work in a guest-service capacity. Service-learning experiences provide students with many opportunities.

Putting It All Together

Few activities in life, including work in the hospitality industry, involve just one of Gardner's intelligences. Instead, many are used together to perform tasks. Therefore, designing courses that provide a wide variety of meaningful activities makes sense for hospitality educators at any level. Indeed, because service-learning taps so many intelligences, it helps facilitate an impressive list of educational benefits. These include:
- increased retention
- high-quality educational opportunities
- increased relevance
- exposure to positive values
- empowerment as learners, teachers, achievers, and leaders
- an invitation to become part of the community
- job skills and preparation
  (University of Colorado n.d.)

In addition, good experiences may positively influence
- problem solving and critical thinking
- ethical development and moral reasoning
- social and civic responsibility
- self-esteem, assertiveness, and empathy
- political efficacy
- tolerance and acceptance of diversity
- career exploration
(National Council for the Social Studies 2000)

Finally, service-learning helps students move beyond the fragmentary work of traditional courses and teaches them instead to deal with an integrated content that reflects the way in which real organizations work. Students learn to act and think like managers in hands-on situations.

Partnership Checklist

Useful tools in collaboration	Yes	No
Self-assessment of curriculum: Where are the service-learning opportunities most applicable? Have they been defined? Do they supplement or facilitate course content and objectives?		
Faculty and staff assessment of course needs: Do faculty members need and want to use service-learning?		
Planning format: Is there a database of successful and less successful service-learning experiences? Are there local contacts? Have the relevant names, contacts, departments, etc. been identified?		
Needs/overlap analysis: Is there a tracking mechanism to ensure that resources are not overtaxed and overused?		
Community job description: What is the community's role in the learning process? Have the community's benefits been identified?		
Information packet for partners: Has a detailed list of interaction opportunities for businesses, agencies, internships, and service-learning projects been developed?		
Working with the community partner: Have project objectives been explained? Have semester or students' constraints been identified?		
Self-assessment: Are service-learning partnership objectives documented?		
Logistics: Have transportation issues been identified? Has the size of student groups been communicated? Has the level of preparation of the students been explained? Have risk releases been obtained?		

(Adapted from Teach 2000 [2000] and Henry 2001)

Attracting Service-Learning Partners

Effective service-learning experiences require faculty members to create alliances with external organizations and entities in the community. Educators should consider the partner's resources and how they might best complement their course or program. Service-learning partnerships can act as a cornerstone for complex growth, bringing together groups not previously allied.

Indeed, the hospitality and tourism fields give faculty members many opportunities to interact with professionals and community residents. Key contacts in the development of a partnership may be a Chamber of Commerce or a visitors' bureau, or an economic development council, as well as traditional service organizations. The checklist is provided to help instructors assess the relevance of developing a service-learning partnership.

Hospitality educators are fortunate to have such varied resources to increase student learning. Sometimes, however, it is difficult to access these resources and organize service-learning activities (O'Halloran, Rolfs, and O'Halloran 2001). Below is a list of strategies that hospitality educators could use to implement service-learning in their courses.

- Brainstorm with colleagues to identify service-learning activities that may be useful. Think outside of the box to generate a list. If a genuine brainstorming exercise is used, then all ideas should initially be accepted. Keep the brainstorming list for future reference.

- Conduct a similar brainstorming activity with students in hospitality classes. Students may have unique hospitality-related experiences or connections that add to the curriculum.

- Develop a community resource file that includes names, phone numbers, email addresses, and street addresses of people to contact at each site.

- Keep a record of which resources have been used, and when, and include a brief evaluation of the activity. Include the positive points of the experience and the areas that should be improved if the resource is to be used again.

- Work with colleagues to avoid duplicating experiences and sites. Share ideas and opportunities and coordinate the use of resources throughout the hospitality curriculum if possible.

- Think about how the community resource may be used most effectively. For example, if a field trip is planned, have a specific purpose in mind and convey that purpose to the students and to the people involved. Try to go beyond the usual tour of a facility to involve the students in some aspect of the operation to increase their learning and add interest to the experience.

Project Overview

Project Title	Content Area	Service	Service-Learning Partner
Nutrition Education	Nutrition principles	Teaching nutrition to children/ education	Denver Public Schools, Girl Scouts,day care centers
Kids' Cuisine	Food preparation and evaluation	Introducing new foods to children/education	Denver Public Schools
Food Safety Education	Sanitation	Sanitation and food handling practices/educa-tion and health	Plattsburgh City Schools
Picketwire Canyon: Dinosaurs for Tourism	Tourism planning	Sustainable development planning and ecotourism	USDA Forest Service, Rocky Mountain Region, Picketwire Canyon
Mt. Evans: Code of Ethics for Visitors	Tourism planning, ethics	Sustainable development	USDA Forest Service: Mt.Evans
Think Like an Owner	Lodging, opera-tions, develop-ment, asset management	Facilitate (lodging) development and economic development	City of Plattsburgh, NY Community Development
Lodging Owner or Manager Recruitment Guide	Recruitment and staffing	Employee recruitment guide	Colorado Hotel & Lodging Association
Redesign of High School Cafeteria	Revitalization of school foodservice	Planning redesign of a high school cafeteria	East High School, Denver Public Schools
Battle of Plattsburgh War Museum	Development of a tourism attraction for the North Country	Assisting development of a nonprofit association	Battle of Plattsburgh Association

Since, moreover, projects are typically linked to specific curricular areas, such areas are explicitly identified in the second column of the facing overview.

The remainder of this chapter highlights the objectives of four of these projects, along with reactions to them and evaluation of them. A profile of other service-learning projects the authors have developed is included in outline form in Attachment A.

Nutrition Education Project

Since many families now eat out regularly, restaurant operators find that serving nutritious, healthy, delicious menu items and providing a family-friendly atmosphere are more important than in the past. These trends were the catalyst for a nutrition education project. The instructor introduced the project to the class as follows:

> It has been said that one of the best ways to learn something is to teach it to someone else. With this in mind, a group of students will be required to complete a presentation on nutrition to schoolchildren. The children have been selected because they are a friendly audience, they are easily accessible, and they provide you with an opportunity to practice presentation skills and to reinforce nutrition course content in a non-threatening environment while adding a sound educational component to the elementary school curriculum. (O'Halloran and O'Halloran 1999)

The instructions given to the students included time line and work expectations. The students were told that it was up to them to schedule their presentation with the classroom teacher (and class) assigned to them. In addition, they were made aware of how they would be evaluated. In this case, the classroom teacher and students would use an evaluation form specifically developed for the project. The project would also be assessed through self- and peer evaluations and through an instructor evaluation of presentation outlines and support media. The students were expected to plan and present the nutrition lessons, taking into consideration their audience and the content materials. This would require careful preparation and collaboration and also reflection on the project activities (Carol Kinsley in Archer 1997).

The university students and the elementary school classes were very positive about this service-learning project. Teacher comments and student evaluations stressed that the key to success was the integration of course content with the service activities. The university students benefited from the initiative by reinforcing their knowledge of nutrition, giving presentations, serving the public schools, and interacting with children. The children gained knowledge of nutrition and had a rare opportunity to interact with college students in a learning situation. Typical student evaluations included comments such as, "It was the best group project I have ever participated in because I felt like we were doing something important," and "I learned a lot about nutrition and we had so much fun with the kids. Can we do it again?" Teacher comments included, "I loved having the college students interact with my students because they really listened to them," and "Opportunities to get these two age groups together and to learn about nutrition at the same time are invaluable." Finally, the children drew pictures of nutritious and favorite foods and provided written feedback, such as, "Carrots are good for your eyes. Eating healthy will make you healthier. I think you did a great job!"

This positive feedback resulted not only from a good initial idea but also from a well-organized follow-through. First, the goals and expectations of the project were clearly outlined for the students and the school personnel. For example, school teachers and youth group leaders were informed that this was a hospitality class and not an education class. Therefore, the focus was on nutrition, and the presentation would use an interpretive model rather than a purely instructional format. An emphasis on working in effective student teams was also part of the project. To this end, the project parameters were clearly outlined; the instructor provided intensive initial guidance; student roles were specified; and project progress was monitored. In addition, a small service-learning grant from the Kettering Family Foundation enabled the hospitality students to offer the children nutritious foods as examples of healthy choices, and to prepare attractive written and visual materials for use in their sessions.

The student activity generated through this program has been exciting and diverse. The presentations have been meaningful to the hospitality students and have contributed significantly to the nutritional knowledge and awareness of the school children and other individuals. For example, one recent project involved making a presentation on nutrition and also writing a booklet on the nutrition of young children for a day care center. The presentation was made to parents and children at a special event, and copies of the booklet were provided to parents and day care staff. Another creative project involved a Brownie Girl Scout troop. Over the course of three troop meetings, the college students helped the girls earn a healthy-food badge through a presentation, interactive games, and the joint preparation of nutritious foods. Numerous projects have focused on presentations to traditional classes at elementary schools. For instance, hospitality students gave a presentation on healthy eating to every class in grades one through five at a nearby school. In addition to providing a community service in nutrition and increasing their own knowledge of nutrition, the students were introduced to interpretation models that helped them to focus on the way in which they communicated their information as well as on its content.

Kids' Cuisine Project

In the Kids' Cuisine project, students designed, created, and tested children's menu items with public elementary school students. The college students visited the schools, interviewed students, and prepared and served creative foods to the children at a special luncheon. The idea behind the project was for the university students to learn about food and basic cooking techniques while offering interesting, healthy food choices that young diners would enjoy. The children's cuisine project incorporated an innovative group project into a traditional course, so that concepts of the course were learned through the topic of children's cuisine. During two two-hour class periods and a laboratory session each week, the students learned about safety and sanitation practices, food products, specifications, recipes, menus, and basic cooking techniques. In addition, they were introduced to survey research techniques to assist them in completing their projects. The students completed a paper for the classroom portion of the course and prepared food for children in the lab.

In addition to the fact that the project reflected demographic and industry trends, it was selected for several complementary reasons. First, it provided the hospitality students with activities well beyond the usual kinds of class assignments. Second, it allowed them to work together on a real-world project, researching, preparing, and serving food to children. Third, it represented a community service and an exciting learning experience for both the students and the children. The hospitality students thrived on their involvement in a real-world project, and the children enjoyed both the attention and the opportunity to sample interesting foods (O'Halloran 1998).

Once the menus were decided upon, the hospitality students planned the preparation and presentation of the food and its evaluation with the help of the chef instructor and the course instructor. Students were responsible for developing the recipes, figuring out their shopping lists, developing food evaluations for the children to complete, preparing and presenting the food, and cleaning up.

The elementary students were then invited to a food tasting at the university. A college classroom was decorated, and children were invited to draw a giant ice cream sundae as they waited for the food tasting to begin. To make the atmosphere especially welcoming, big paper footprints were taped on the building stairs, and menus were posted on the doors to direct the children to the food-tasting room.

The luncheon was served in separate courses, with one team at a time presenting its creation to the children for careful tasting and evaluation. After the tasting, the hospitality students examined the children's feedback, some of which consisted simply of happy faces, and evaluated their own food preparation and presentation activities. Each team wrote a paper that included research on children's cuisine, survey results from their own research with children, sample menus, recipes, and an evaluation of their food project. Finally, each team briefed the class about children's cuisine.

From the surveys and interactions, the hospitality students learned some surprising things about children's eating preferences. For example, a junior majoring in hospitality management stated that, for fourth and fifth graders, "We learned that presentation is really important. The kids we talked to don't want anything that reminds them that they're kids — no dinosaurs on their plates" (Olgeirson 1997). Another student found that a "restaurant atmosphere" is very important to children. She noted that children "love places where they can make their own food and where there is entertainment."

The hospitality students also voiced positive opinions about the project. Several students enjoyed their conversations with the children, the opportunity to come up with creative ideas and then to actually test them, and "how it was more of a live performance than just a written presentation." Another student noted that "this project was helpful because children often are ignored." Students also felt that focusing the project on children increased their awareness of the importance of this market segment.

"Think Like an Owner" Project

"Think Like an Owner" contributed to the economic progress and development plans of a small community in northern New York. Students examined the development and revitalization of the town's waterfront, focusing on the need to spur economic development. The tasks involved in the project included:
- identifying a site
- conducting an area review
- developing a concept
- conducting a competitive analysis for the proposed property
- quantifying demand
- estimating impacts on the community, economically, socially and environmentally, with an emphasis on sustainable development

• estimating the ability of the new property to penetrate the market based on market needs and desires
• defining product level and service
• defining segments to target
• defining a mix of rooms
• defining size
• developing amenities (to be identified as variable-cost or fixed-cost)
• defining furniture, fixture, and equipment decisions
• defining facilities
• determining the costs of development
• estimating annual operating results
• examining comparable market data for forecasting purposes (e.g., per occupied room or per available room comparable)

This project was developed as an integrative exercise, within which students were asked to make many decisions. The goal of the project was for students to develop a concept or renovate an existing property and evaluate its potential for success in a given market. Students had to undertake considerable fieldwork and judge their original ideas and intentions against market demands. As they identified and obtained more data, they could adjust their projects to meet market needs. These decisions had to take into account human resources, staffing, amenities provided, facilities needed, operational systems, and market-positioning. (See Attachment B for the rubric used in this course.) Students were required to present their results in written as well as oral form, but were also allowed to submit their work early for feedback and evaluation as well as to consult with guest experts from the field such as a hotel general manager, a market analyst and appraiser of hotels, and an asset manager.

The results of the project were shared with the community and contributed to its long-range plans for economic and tourism development.

Redesign of High School Cafeteria

In another service-learning project, a school district requested help in revitalizing a high school cafeteria's foodservice program. The students needed to meet with clients, identify and interview representatives from student and faculty target markets, and collect information needed to make decisions. The project lasted for six months and was integrated into two courses. Students collected operating information from the Department of Food and Nutrition Services and then interviewed all the stakeholders at the high school. Data collection included surveys and focus groups consisting of high school students, teachers, administrators, food and nutrition employees, and local quick-service restaurant operators. Students analyzed the results and made recommendations to the school and the district. Their final results were then presented to the director of foodservice and nutrition and the chief operating officer for the school district.

All the recommendations of the students were accepted, including a redesign of the cafeteria, a project budgeted at approximately $80,000 that was carried through to completion, including the hiring of one of the students to lead the undertaking. Use of the improved facility grew from 70 students per day to more than 400. Clearly, this was a win-win situation for all involved. Thanks to the project's success, one student was offered a position in the district to implement similar programs citywide. The cafeteria redesign and related results were featured in *Food Management* magazine, and the class wrote a teaching case study that is being used in a contract management class. Since the district had to examine the recommendations from a cost-benefit standpoint, adoption of the project represented a major validation of the students' efforts.

Conclusion

Service-learning involves much more than organizing a project. It represents a commitment to the creation of learning opportunities for students. Not all students learn in the same way, and not all instructors teach in the same manner. Service-learning provides both faculty and students with an exciting and rigorous pedagogy that strengthens the ties between academic and real-world practice. Service-learning can be an integral part of a business education. The partnerships it builds, when designed and operated effectively, can enhance quality and capitalize on the strengths of the hospitality and tourism industry's many and diverse stakeholders.

Service-learning also provides opportunities for reflection on the connections between the service experience, democratic values, and citizenship. In short, service-learning represents good education, good business, and a community benefit. Truly effective service-learning projects go beyond simply providing a vehicle for student development. They also seek to solve real community problems, meet important human and environmental needs, and advocate for changes in policies and laws to promote the common good (National Council for the Social Studies 2000).

Attachment A. Service-Learning Profiles

Project Name: Food Safety Education

Partner(s): Denver Public Schools, Plattsburgh City Schools

Organization Liaison: classroom teachers

Project Objective(s): food safety content knowledge enhanced, presentation skills, know your audience

Type (content) of Project: consumer education

Detailed Description of Project: presentation of food safety and sanitation content to elementary students

Outcomes for Students: improved presentation and comprehension of food safety content

Scope of Project: teach classes in Plattsburgh City Schools

Geographic Location: Plattsburgh, NY, Momont Elementary School, Denver, CO

Deliverable Product: lesson for class

Project Name: Battle of Plattsburgh War Museum

Partner(s): Battle of Plattsburgh War Museum Association, NY Assemblyman's office

Organization Liaison: President of the Association

Project Objective(s): create ideas and alternative activities and attractions to make the museum economically and demand viable

Type (content) of Project: will create 8 different scenarios and ideas for proposed museum

Detailed Description of Project: presentation of creative ideas to develop the museum, including attractions, interpretation, funding sources

Outcomes for Students: research skills, creativity exercise

Scope of Project: assist association in planning and development process

Geographic Location: Plattsburgh, NY

Deliverable Product: student reports

Project components: statement of product, literature review, comparable locations, area review, recommendations, partnerships, funding

Industry Segments Served: cultural and historical tourism in the North Country

Project Name: Employee Recruitment Guide for Owners

Partner(s): Colorado Hotel & Lodging Association

Organization Liaison: Executive Director of the Association

Project Objective(s): locate and assimilate data for lodging owners and managers

Type (content) of Project: guidebook to assist small lodging operators to recruit, attract, and retain employees in a difficult labor market

Detailed Description of Project: guide for lodging owners and managers, targeted to smaller operators

Outcomes for Students: primary and secondary research skills, Internet use, presentation skills

Scope of Project: students conducted primary research and presented results

Geographic Location: Denver, CO

Deliverable Product: user guide

Industry Segments Served: lodging and resort

Project Considerations: timing was an issue for completion of project

Project Name: Mt. Evans Visitor Ethics Plan & Commercial Use Plan

Partner(s): USDA Forest Service, Rocky Mountain Region

Organization Liaison: District Ranger, Public Relations Officer, Recreation Team

Project Objectives(s): develop a plan for making Mt. Evans a sustainable tourism resource, including visitor code of ethics and recommendations for commercial use

Type (content) of Project: field research, primary research interviews, work with USDA representatives, work with stakeholder groups

Detailed Description of Project: plan developed and recommendation made by students for fees and commercial use; recreation use restrictions and visitor ethics code developed

Outcomes for Students: research, primary and secondary; communication skills with stakeholder groups, consensus building

Geographic Location: Denver and Lakewood, CO, Mt. Evans region

Deliverable Product: formal written plans and presentations

Industry Segments Served: tourism, recreation businesses, local communities

Project Evaluation Procedures: instructor evaluation of reports and presentations, evaluation by client and other stakeholders

Project Considerations/Advice & Observations: project very successful using a mix of graduate and undergraduate students

Project Name: Picketwire Canyon Development

Partner(s): USDA Forest Service, Rocky Mountain Region

Organization Liaison: District Ranger, Public Relations Officer, Recreation Team

Project Objectives(s): write plan for development of Picketwire Canyon

Type (content) of Project: field research, primary research interviews, work with USDA representatives, work with stakeholder groups

Detailed Description of Project: plan developed and recommendation made by students for infrastructure, transportation, and recreation use

Outcomes for Students: research, primary and secondary; communication skills with stakeholder groups; consensus building

Geographic Location: Denver and Lakewood, CO, southeastern Colorado

Deliverable Product: formal written plans and presentations

Industry Segments Served: tourism, recreation businesses, and local communities

Project Evaluation Procedures: instructor evaluation of reports and presentations, evaluation by client and other stakeholders

Attachment B. Project Rubric

Project Evaluation 300 points /240 points paper/60 points presentation
(presentation rubric not included)

	Possible Points	Your Score

Professional presentation   5
Projects are expected to be complet-
ed and submitted in a professional
manner. The framework for this
should be to turn the project into a
community development organization or potential investor for funding
consideration.

Organization   5
Organization and flow of the project
is also expected to be logical. The
topics should flow from one to the
other with the subjects related and
presented with the use of good transition statements and justifications.

Grammar & spelling   5
This area is expected to be proof-
read.

Description of subject property   5
Present a detailed profile of your
concept, its features and the benefits for prospective guests and the
community. What will your product
look like? What amenities will be
included? What items will be considered a variable cost? Which
items are fixed cost? How much
will it cost to completely furnish
your rooms?

	Possible Points	Your Score

Site evaluation   10

Note your site by address, region etc. and evaluate it based on the old saying "Location! Location! Location!" What are the physical, environmental, social and financial implications for the community?

Area review   20

What are the markets and economic factors that impact or influence demand for room nights in your market? How do they relate to growth of demand? Can demand be created?

Competitive supply analysis   20

Who are your competitors, how were they selected, why are they competitive? What data has been selected and what does your analysis indicate?

Growth of demand analysis   20

How will the market behave in the future based on the indicators that you have identified? This should be explained by segment.

Penetration analysis   30

How will your property enter the market and compete with existing hotels? What is your fair share? Can you estimate your penetration rate and justify how you will achieve it?

Rate analysis   20

What is your product mix and what rates will you charge? Included is a discussion of rack rates, discounts per segments, group sales, etc.

Estimated operating results   20
Estimate operating results for a representative year at the proposed property. Forecast revenues and examine comparable properties for estimation of expenses, etc. Are your expenses based on Per Occupied Room, or Per Available Room, Fixed Cost vs. Variable Cost?

Operational decision making   35
What decisions can you make about the day-to-day operation of your property? These decisions are human resources, staffing, scheduling, market positioning, technological tools, etc.

Justification of decisions   35
Why are your decisions correct? Have you related your decisions to the market data and creation of products? Where did you get the information? References listed?

Conclusions   10
What are your estimated development and construction costs, what is the ROI? What is the payback period? An assessment of community tax benefits is also helpful.

Did you have to change your concept based on market data as your project progressed?

Total Points

Feedback:

(O'Halloran 2000)

References

Archer, J. (May 14, 1997). "Students Need Help Meeting Service Mandates, Study Says." *Education Week on the Web.* www.edweek.org/htbin/fastwe...doc+view4+ew1997+886+0+wAAA+%26%28.

Donovan, B., and R. Iovino. (October 1997). "A 'Multiple Intelligences' Approach to Expanding and Celebrating Teacher Portfolios and Student Portfolios." Paper presented at the Annual Meeting of the Northeastern Educational Research Association.

Gardner, H. (1983). *Frames of Mind: The Theory of Multiple Intelligences.* New York: Basic Books.

_____. (2003). "Reinventing our Schools: A Conversation with Howard Gardner, 1994." http://www.ed.psu/insys/ESD/gardner/Assess.html.

Henry, R. (2001). "Service-Learning: Campus and Community Collaboration: From Shibboleth to Reality." www.mc.maricopa.edu/academic/compact/rhenryop.html, 1-14.

Hoyt, B., and J. Thalman. (Jan.-March 2001). "Service-Learning as a Training Platform for Business Tomorrow." *Webnet Journal* 3 (i):16.

National Council for the Social Studies. (May 2000). "Service-Learning: An Essential Component of Citizenship Education. http://web6.infotrac.galegroup.com.

National Service-Learning Cooperative Clearinghouse, An Adjunct ERIC Clearinghouse on Service-Learning, Impacts and Effects of Service-Learning. www.nicsl.coled.umn.edu/Bibliographies_HTML/impacts/intro.htm.

O'Halloran, C.S. (1998). "Catering to Children as a Class Project." *Journal of Hospitality & Tourism Education* 9 (4): 52-55.

O'Halloran, C.S., R. Rolfs, and R. O'Halloran. (2001). "Using Community Resources to Make Learning More Meaningful: Assessing Rural Educational Settings." *Journal of Hospitality & Tourism Education* 13 (5): 51-57.

O'Halloran, R.M. (2000). Unpublished course syllabus for HRTM 384 *Hospitality Finance,* SUNY Plattsburgh.

O'Halloran, R.M., and C.S. O'Halloran. (1999). "Nutrition Education: The Interpretive Model." *Journal of Hospitality & Tourism Education* 11 (1):19-21.

Olgeirson, A. (March 1997). "Elementary Student Testers Say 'Mikey Likes It.'" *The Source* 18 (5): p. 1.

Teach 2000. The Educator's Guide to the Internet and World Wide Web. (2000). "Pedagogical Perspectives: The Pedagogy of Technology." www.lhbe.edu.on.ca/teach2000/classroom/pedagogy.html.

Tucker, M. L., and A.M. McCarthy. (Summer 2001). "Presentation Self-Efficacy: Increasing Communication Skills through Service-Learning." *Journal of Managerial Issues* 13 (2): 227.

Tucker, M.L., A.M. McCarthy, J. Hoxmeier, and M. Link (1998). "Community Service-Learning Increases Communication Skills across Business Curriculum." *Business Communication Quarterly* 61: 89-100.

University of Colorado. (n.d.). "Benefits of Service-Learning." http://csf.colorado.edu/sl/benefits/html.

Service-Learning Projects for Extra Credit

by Nancy Swanger

Introduction

As I was putting together the materials to teach an introductory course in hospitality for the first time, during fall 2001, I spent a lot of time trying to decide on appropriate extra-credit opportunities for the students. After much deliberation, I decided that, since service was at the very heart of any career in the hospitality field, gaining experience in being of service to others would be beneficial for all involved. After the events of September 11, the idea of serving others took on a whole new meaning and further emphasized the importance of being of service to others. Upon polling the students on the first day of class, I found that only about one third had worked in the hospitality industry or in any service-related job. This helped validate my idea that the earning of extra credit needed to involve service for the benefit of others.

The hospitality industry has long been known for its generosity — during good times and bad. Most recently, on October 11, 2001, more than 8,000 restaurants contributed $21 million to relief efforts through Dine Out for America and Windows of Hope (National Restaurant Association 2001a). In addition, the New York Marriott Financial Center Hotel, while sustaining major damage and closure as a result of the Trade Center attacks, made itself available for a Red Cross relief station.

On a more routine note, Marriott International sponsors its annual Spirit to Serve Our Communities Day, when Marriott associates participate in projects that benefit Habitat for Humanity, the elderly, the ill, and many others (Marriott 2001). The National Restaurant Association (2001b) supports the Restaurant Good Neighbor Award to recognize owners and operators who make a difference in their local communities. A finalist for the Restaurant Good Neighbor Award from the state of Washington was the Sawtooth Grill in Spokane, which provides support to the Spokane Centennial Trail. The restaurant donated $1 from the sale of every Centennial Fudge Cake and adopted Mile 37 of the trail for maintenance. Volunteers from the restaurant's staff and management take care of Mile 37, and over $10,000 (22 percent of the Trail's annual budget) has been contributed thus far. I am proud to point out that two of the restaurant's managers are graduates of the Hotel and Restaurant Administration Program at Washington State University. These are just a few of the countless examples where members of the hospitality industry have stepped up to serve their community.

Service-learning has been characterized as "an increasingly popular pedagogy that integrates community service into an organized curriculum that includes regular opportunities for personal reflection" (Andersen 1998). Furthermore, as part of the hospitality curriculum, it is not new; a few schools like Cornell and the University of Houston have been using it for years. However, it appears from the literature that most of the hospitality courses incorporating service-learning have been offered at the upper-division, capstone, or graduate levels (DeFranco and Abbott 1996; Stevens 1997/1998; Kim 1999; Stevens 1999), not as part of the first course in the curriculum. I was unable to find research that discussed using service-learning as an extra-credit opportunity, at any level.

In this essay, I will describe my fall 2001 project as it evolved during the semester, and what I learned about service-learning. I will conclude with a description of the changes I planned to implement during the fall 2002 semester.

Extra Credit in HA 181 (Introduction to Hospitality) – Fall 2001

The introductory course was structured to have 500 possible total points, resulting from group projects, pop quizzes, and tests. On the first day of class, each student was given a syllabus outlining the structure of the course. Among other things, a sheet (Figure 1) was included describing the only extra-credit opportunity available, and I explained the rationale behind its selection.

Figure 1. Extra-Credit Opportunities

HA 181 – Extra-Credit
Service-Learning Project

The essence of the hospitality industry is service—service to others, internal and external customers alike. As a way of learning what it means to truly be of service to others, the following extra-credit opportunity is available:

WHO: HA 181 students wanting extra credit.

WHAT: Participate in work for people or agencies in need of help. Students will earn **5 extra-credit points per hour** of service **(50 points maximum)** for the semester.

WHEN: Anytime that works for the student and those in need of help.

WHERE: With any person or organization willing to accept some help. Suggestions include, but are not limited to: working at the food bank, giving time to any United Way or other non-profit civic agency, visiting folks in a nursing home, reading to/with elementary-age children, helping with community clean-up or service projects, walking dogs at the animal shelter, or anything else you think would qualify. If you are unsure, just ask! Projects you might already be involved in with other people, such as through your living group or a club, do not qualify.

HOW: Representatives from the Community Service-learning Center (CSLC) will be in class to explain their programs and how to get involved through them. You may also contact a person or organization, on your own, that you wish to serve and make the necessary arrangements. Complete your assignment and fill out the "HA 181 – Extra-credit" form and turn in it to Nancy on or before **[date]**.

WHY: Because it's a good thing to do—and the only way to earn extra credit in HA 181!

I also included the documentation sheet (Figure 2) required for awarding the points.

Figure 2. Extra-Credit Documentation

HA 181 EXTRA-CREDIT - SERVICE-LEARNING DOCUMENTATION		
NAME: ID #: SECTION:		
ORGANIZATION: CONTACT: PHONE #:		
DATE(S) OF SERVICE: HOUR(S) OF SERVICE:		
DESCRIPTION OF SERVICES PROVIDED:		
COMMENTS FROM PERSON(S)/AGENCY SERVED:		
SIGNATURE: PRINTED NAME:		
PHONE NUMBER: DATE:		
PERSONAL REFLECTION OF SERVICE-LEARNING EXPERIENCE:		
SIGNATURE: PRINTED NAME:		

Through service work, students were allowed to earn up to 50 extra-credit points (5 points earned per hour of service), which could amount to 10 percent of the total possible points, or one full letter grade. Each student was responsible for arranging their own placement, although I provided a few suggestions. The goal was to have individual students help persons or agencies that were in need. Students were not allowed to count hours worked through a pre-arranged club or living-group activity. In other words, if a student's sorority participated in the annual clean-up project on campus, those hours were not awarded extra-credit points. Students were also required to submit the completed documentation form to me by the assigned due date. If the form was incomplete in any way, they had to correct what was missing and resubmit.

Results. Of the 149 students enrolled in HA 181 during the fall 2001 semester, 79 (53 percent) participated in the extra-credit opportunity. In total, the students provided 859 hours of service. Of the 79 participants, 26 (33 percent) spent more than 10 hours helping, even though they were awarded extra-credit points only up to 10 hours. These 26 students logged a total of 412 hours, which was 48 percent of the total hours. The number of hours ranged from 2 to 50+. Table 1 shows most of the organizations served by the students.

Table 1. Persons or Agencies Served by HA 181 Students - Fall 2001

Hospice	Public Schools
Pen Friends	YMCA
Children's Centers	Women's Transit
Humane Society	Police Department
Sigma Iota	Union Gospel Mission
Nursing/Retirement Centers	Food Banks
Campfire Boys & Girls	American Cancer Society
Ski For All Foundation	World Concern
Red Cross	Various Community Clean-up Projects

In reading the personal reflection section on each student's documentation form, I was struck by the number who said they had been reluctant to participate but had had such a good experience that they would participate again, even without extra-credit points attached. Several students (13 percent) planned to continue their service after returning from the semester break. Table 2 shows some of the comments made by students as they reflected on their experiences.

Table 2. Student Comments on Their Service-Learning Experience

"The food bank was a good experience. It felt like I was working at a store like I have in the past, by taking out carts and handling food. It felt good that I was helping people in need and who were less fortunate."

"I believe that volunteering for the Campfire Boys and Girls organization was a great experience. It was a lot of fun and gave me a chance to interact with kids, which I don't get a chance to do very often. I would be more than willing to volunteer my help to them anytime I could."

"I felt this service project was the most rewarding because we were helping older people do work that more than likely would not be done if we weren't there. . . . I would do this again if given the opportunity!"

"Another thing that blew me away was the people. They were there every day from 8-4 volunteering their time for the sake of other people. That really impressed me. Their lives were totally devoted to service."

"From doing this work I feel better about living in Pullman. I feel that doing this service, I'm giving something back to the community."

Table 3 shows some of the comments by agency personnel who worked with the students during the semester.

Table 3. Agency Personnel Comments on Student Service Learning Contributions

"Kanako was one of the most dedicated volunteers I had. She never missed a meeting and showed up every time we were working. She put in a lot of hard work for many hours. I would like to work with her again."

"He did an outstanding job, with an eager attitude to learn. He was willing to be uncomfortable for the sake of taking on a 'learning experience.' I was very impressed."

"Abbie has been an excellent volunteer for Women's Transit. She has been reliable, followed procedures properly, and provided a service to keep women safe on campus and throughout Pullman."

"David worked with students with specific learning disabilities and students with developmental disabilities. He assisted students on the computer completing assignments, walked with students around the track, graded papers, helped at lunch. He did a terrific job!"

"Analia was a very helpful and cheery volunteer. She was wonderful with the guests. We all enjoyed her help. I am very pleased to have had her donate her time and would be happy if she returned for the next conference!"

"It is always a pleasure to have Ashley in my classroom. She is very helpful and has a great rapport with the children. She always responds to them in a positive way and makes each one feel special."

"Our patients' ages range from 40 to 86 years; they dialyze three times a week, averaging four hours per dialysis. Boredom is ever-present despite TV. Katie is a breath of fresh air! Patients look forward to her visits, her tales, and sharing with her."

Lessons Learned

After all the extra-credit forms were collected, the points awarded, and the final grades submitted, I had a chance to meet with Troy Robey and Melanie Brown, the key persons in the Community Service-Learning Center (CSLC) at Washington State University. During this meeting (Robey 2001; Brown 2001) I learned the following:

• CSLC's definition of service-learning focuses on the benefit provided to an underserved population or individual, or the common good. This includes direct contact or connection with people, or possibly animals, and goes beyond just the planning of an event. It may also include participation as an advocate for the underserved.

• In true service-learning, the recipient and the provider of the service benefit equally.

• To qualify as service-learning, the participants need objectives that identify what they hope to get out of the experience.

• One difference between community service and service-learning is the reflective piece completed by the service-provider. One suggestion was to have students submit a one-page reflection or journal entry for each visit. In their reflections, students describe what they feel and what they have learned with regard to themselves, their community, and their major or career path.

• The word volunteer is not used in print or speaking; this helps distinguish service-learning from community service. Instead, the word participant is used whenever possible.

• At the end of the semester, students are brought together with a facilitator for group reflection sessions and celebration.

This information is consistent with information I received via email from Tom Van Dyke (2001):

I view service-learning as having four components: 1) Pre-service training based upon an academic curriculum that is project specific. 2) Meaningful service based upon the unmet needs of the community and developmentally appropriate for the students. 3) Structured post-service reflection where students are able to discuss the problems faced and their efforts to make a difference. Reflection usually involves a journal where students are able to write about their feelings and ideas. 4) A celebration where students are recognized for the work they have accomplished and encouraged to continue their service (Fertman 1994).

Organizational Support for Service-Learning Classes

Although the CSLC office at Washington State University is rather small — one full-time program director and a handful of part-time graduate assistants — there is a significant amount of support for faculty looking to incorporate service-learning into their courses.

The office makes staff available to discuss options with faculty, as well as to visit classes to explain the service-learning program (overview, benefits, procedures) to students. CSLC will also review a course syllabus to help the instructor create a learning experience that aligns with course objectives. Programs can be tailored for groups as well as individuals, with an extensive database of participating community partners for students to choose from. The CSLC office conducts orientation and placement sessions that provide students with detailed information on how the program works. The office keeps track of the number of hours each student participates and forwards that information to the instructor via an Excel spreadsheet. Students have the option of continuing their service, and the CSLC office hosts reflective sessions in which students can share and evaluate their experience. Students who complete eight or more hours of service receive a transcript of their work.

The office also makes available an extensive list of resources and contacts for faculty and students who wish to learn more about service-learning and its components. Washington State University is a member of the Washington Campus Compact, whose purpose is to educate and support member schools in promoting service-learning as part of the curriculum. Other members include Gonzaga University, Seattle Central Community College, University of Washington, and Western Washington University.

Service-Learning for Extra Credit in HA 181 — Fall 2002

To make the HA 181 extra-credit opportunity a true service-learning project, I decided to implement the following changes for the fall semester:

• Schedule an in-class presentation, during the first week of the semester, with CSLC speakers to explain the process and their role in the service-learning experience.

• Require students choosing to work with CSLC staff or agencies to attend a placement session for selection and assignment of their experience. Assignments would match the needs of the underserved with the interests, talents, and schedules of the student.

• Require those opting to earn extra credit to submit their first journal entry prior to midterm. It would describe where and whom they will be serving, their feelings at the start, and a brief plan of their activities. (Although meaningful service-learning can take place through a single experience, I prefer that students put some thought and planning into their service work rather than wait until the last minute and take whatever is available to accumulate the required hours.)

• Require students to keep a journal on their participation and submit their entries, together with the service-learning documentation form, by the due date.

• Require students to participate in a post-experience celebration. (The Washington State University CSLC hosts a campuswide reception that includes a poster presentation of some of the semester's projects, as well as an awards ceremony recognizing contributors to the service-learning effort. Distinguished Service-Learning Awards are presented to a student, a faculty member, and a community agency by university officials, such as the academic provost and the vice-president of student affairs. Toward the end of the semester, the CSLC also schedules reflective sessions for students and faculty who have participated in service-learning projects.)

Conclusion

Although my first attempt at incorporating service-learning for extra credit in an introductory hospitality class was less than perfect, I believe the students won, the people or agencies served won, the involved communities won, and Washington State University and its department of Hotel and Restaurant Administration definitely won. As I noted earlier, a sampling of the comments from the students and the agencies they served indicates how beneficial the experience was to those involved. Whenever students are out providing meaningful service to the local community, their work can only serve to enhance the image of the school and its students, and the development of a strong campus/community relationship. By graduating students who are technically and academically prepared, as well as aware of what it means truly to be a part of a community, institutions of higher learning garner continued support from the constituents they serve.

References

Andersen, S.M. (1998). "Service-Learning: A National Strategy for Youth Development." www.gwu.edu/~ccps/pop_svc.html.

Brown, M. (Dec 14, 2001). Personal interview.

DeFranco, A.L., and J.L. Abbott. (1996). "Teaching Community Service and the Importance of Citizenry." *Hospitality & Tourism Educator* 8 (1): 5-7.

Fertman, C.I. (1994). *Service-Learning for All Students.* Bloomington, IN: Phi Delta Kappa Educational Foundation.

Kim, H.Y. (1999). "Giving a Helping Hand to a Hunger Program: Combining Service-Learning and Managerial Communication Basics." *Journal of Hospitality & Tourism Education* 11 (2/3): 22-24.

Marriott International. (2001). Photo Archive — Marriott Newsroom. www.marriot-tnewsroom.com/photolibrary.asp?brand=photo.

National Restaurant Association. (2001a). "World Trade Center, Pentagon Tragedies Prompt Restaurant Industry Response." http://restaurant.org/news/response.cfm.

_____. (2001b). "Restaurant Neighbor Award 2001 Winners." www.restaurant.org/cornerstone/ma/RNA_profile.cfm?ID=77.

Robey, T. (Dec. 14, 2001). Interview.

Stevens, B. (1999). "Fostering Volunteerism: A Course in Managerial Communication and Ethics." *Journal of Hospitality & Tourism Education* 11 (2/3): 50-53.

_____. (1997/1998). "Service-Learning: Merging Hospitality and Volunteerism." *Journal of Hospitality & Tourism Education* 9 (4): 63-65.

Van Dyke, T. (Oct. 26, 2001). Email correspondence.

From Volunteerism to Service-Learning:
A Recipe for the Success of Foodservice Education

by Keith H. Mandabach

Introduction

Our industry has a major impact on the lives of all we touch. Be it the sanitation, taste, and nutrition of the food we serve, the quality of service, or the ambience of the venue, the foodservice industry has the potential to affect the lives of almost every human being. Hence, it would be hard to overestimate the importance of finding a way for hospitality and foodservice education to contribute more effectively to the improvement of basic human needs (Hegarty 1990). Volunteer work has been, traditionally, the most popular response, but its results are often mixed. By moving to a structured service-learning program, educators can avoid some of the problems common to volunteer work, but only if such a program is designed to clearly communicate its goals and benefits. Involvement in service-learning activities should enable students to improve their technical skills, develop pride in their profession, and reflect on the connection between their efforts and the community's well-being. These activities, it is hoped, will ingrain a habit of community service. Service-learning can also benefit foodservice programs themselves through the positive publicity it generates.

"Purpose" and "reflection" are two key components in this kind of work. Students need to understand that the industry has a history of responding to the community both as a supplier of food for charity events and on an individual level. The late Herman Rusch, fabled chef of the Greenbriar Resort, once declared (Brown 1982), "Every chef must be a gentleman or gentlewoman." By this he meant that every chef must have principles and subscribe to the ethics expressed in the 1957 Culinarians' Code of the American Culinary Federation (2002). That code begins, "I pledge my professional knowledge and skill to the advancement of our profession and to pass it on to those who are to follow." Nine other pledges follow, and all are designed to contribute to the growth of the foodservice profession. The code implies a dedication to mentorship and a commitment to something higher than just serving food. While Rusch's terminology may be out of date, his philosophy of contributing to the community is not.

The Group Learning Connection

It takes a team to produce a meal, and the service-learning activities that take place in our discipline can only produce positive results if participants interact effectively. Michaelson et al. (1996: 373-397) note this requires ongoing accountability (both individual and group). Assignments must be linked and mutually reinforcing, and the process must include practices that stimulate idea exchange. Links can best be created by establishing a vision and purpose for the planned activity during pre-service training. Too often the importance of each individual's effort and contribution is overlooked in a rush to assemble enough people to staff an event. Synergy and a sense of mutual appreciation are often casualties of this approach.

Most foodservice educators, including me, have experienced student discontent with experiential learning activities. However, a thoughtful, well-planned service-learning project can help students establish important connections to their future profession and the community. The risks of including a service-learning component are well worth the effort. Developing a structure for these activities assists the educator in avoiding numerous pitfalls. Perhaps the most critical element in the transition from volunteerism to service-learning involves providing clear opportunities for reflection and an exchange of ideas (Clark 2000). Where volunteerism becomes service-learning is the point of effective reflection.

Foodservice Education Overview

American foodservice education developed from the formal European apprenticeship systems that, in turn, had their roots in the medieval guilds (Baskette 2000: 7). While universities and culinary schools provide intensive training, an essential "finishing" component of foodservice education remains the "rite of passage": working long hours in hot kitchens under the individual supervision of an experienced professional (Dornenburg and Page 1996: 117). Needless to say, special bonds arise between the novice and the mentor. Such bonding affects foodservice education in three ways. First, educators often have very strong relationships with former mentors. Second, educators try to develop the same kind of relationships with their students. Third, many of the educators involve their students in volunteer projects because they themselves participated in such projects during their own training. In addition, they often have connections with former chef mentors still involved in volunteer events.

Chefs have been volunteering in the community for more than 150 years. Chef Charles Senn fed the homeless in London in the

1850s, and Charles Ranhoffer did the same in the panic of 1886 in New York (Crosby 1994). The American Culinary Federation has an entire branch of its organization dedicated to charity: the Chef and Child Foundation (2002). This organization documents how chefs are contributing to efforts to improve the environment, recycle food for food banks, and collect necessities for the homeless.

Hospitality firms are often invited to participate in charitable undertakings by donating funds for the preparation and servicing of an event. Industry owners and managers are advised to participate in public-service activities because of their public-relations value, but are also warned that publicity must be planned to be effective (Morrison 1996: 475). In addition to hosting charity events, the industry provides a venue where the community can discuss important issues; for example, when it hosts service clubs such as Rotary International and Kiwanis. Communities raise funds for charities using industry talent and facilities.

Clearly, working in foodservice is more than just preparing and cooking food. By its very nature, it is experiential and requires interaction with customers and communities. When students participate in community activities through service-learning, they are able to understand not only the intricacies of foodservice but also the way in which the industry contributes to the community.

Foodservice education itself has a long history of volunteerism and service-learning. Seventy years ago, pioneer professional foodservice programs and students and faculty members volunteered their expertise in helping with community and school events. These early programs, developed under the Smith-Hughes Vocational Education Act in the 1920s and 1930s, were based on a combination of classroom and hands-on training (Lapp 1941: 33-45). The programs enabled students to contribute to their school and community in a variety of ways.

Students of Alice McDonald at the Frank Wiggins Trade School (now LA Trade Tech) volunteered at benefits in Hollywood and hosted lunches for school events in 1929 (Staff 1933). The Oakland Trade Schools (now Laney Tech) volunteered at chef association events (Hamesfahr 1934), and Auguste Forster's students at Washburne in Chicago volunteered at the National Restaurant Association Show in 1941 (Willy 1941), as well as participating in activities supporting the war effort throughout the early 1940s (Johnson 1943). Arnold Shircliffe, a pioneer lecturer at Cornell, an instructor at Washburne, and a friend of Forster, stressed the importance of contributing to the community in a book written for the U.S. Navy (Shircliffe 1943). The pioneering efforts at these schools are continuing today in technical colleges, community colleges, culinary schools, and universities (Mandabach 2002).

Adding New Substance to Service

Most service in foodservice education initially occurs as an unstructured afterthought. Educators are requested to provide assistance for school events, charity events, festivals, and other community activities, and they often feel pressured to help out. A community college president or administrator may suggest starting a foodservice program as a great way to receive free catering, and it is difficult for the educator to say no. The results are not always positive for the students or for the education process. An event organizer may set overly high expectations for the students, paid staff may treat the students inappropriately, students may fail to show up, sponsors may expect something for nothing, an event may be poorly organized, or students may view their assigned work as demeaning.

But a more substantive approach is now making its way into foodservice programs. Among numerous examples of projects that have made that transition from volunteerism to service-learning is Cornell University's hunger program (Kim 1999) and Johnson & Wales's culinary program (Sleade 1998). Both demonstrate that service-learning activities should be well-organized and occur in a planned framework that stresses individual student accountability. Not only should student efforts be evaluated, but students should continually evaluate the activities they participate in.

At the University of Denver, a structured service-learning program in a nutrition class produced information that assisted a school district's foodservice in improving the quality of its school lunch program, and at the same time demonstrated the university's commitment to seeking creative learning opportunities for students. As O'Halloran and O'Halloran (1999) note, "Service-learning provides the faculty member and the student with an exciting and rigorous learning methodology that strengthens the tie between academia and industry practice." This article focuses on the value of the student experience while emphasizing the underlying philosophical foundations of the service-learning process.

Service-Learning as Promotion and Recipe

Proposing service-learning for its public-relations value may seem callous, but the examples mentioned above (and countless others not mentioned) probably would not have occurred if the participants had not expected to use the project to promote themselves and their programs. Furthermore, foodservice education has probably gained a good number of students because celebrity chefs have been featured in the media for their involvement in public-service projects.

Administrators enjoy touting their program's accomplishments, and at evaluation time it doesn't hurt an educator to have received positive press.

Most importantly, the service or volunteer project must be done well and produce desirable results. Charity dinners must be gloriously served, the food must be tasty and arrive on time, and the after-dinner cleanup must be thorough. Indeed, to receive the benefits of service-learning projects, those projects must be planned effectively from the start.

While many foodservice educators have the knowledge and experience to serve professional dinners, working with student labor is another experience altogether, educational and with unique issues. Just as a chef preparing a specialty dessert must have not only the ingredients but also a recipe, so the ingredients in a service-learning experience consist of more than just the food — they also include students. Unless learning is part of the equation, students should not be part of the recipe. We must create a new recipe that includes the entire educational process that is service-learning. Before chefs begin, they usually make certain of their "mis en place" (putting things in place). Before beginning the service-learning recipe, it is best to examine the philosophical and curricular foundations of the process, because if everything is not in place before starting, problems will develop.

Philosophical Foundations

A survey of the philosophical foundations underlying service-learning usually starts with the Progressive Movement of the early 20th century and the Humanistic Movement of the 1960s and 1970s. The Progressive Movement gave service-learning its goal of an enlightened citizenry promoting social change through the use of organized scientific inquiry (Dewey 1915). From the humanists has come an emphasis on affective as well as cognitive outcomes, and the goal of producing total human beings (Ornstein and Hunkings 1988). The progressives in the service-learning movement might view positive social change as the primary value of service-learning, but humanists would view development of the total person as the top priority. Interestingly, the reflection that results from the use of Dewey's method of scientific inquiry makes a major contribution to the humanistic self-actualization of participants.

Both of these emphases help shape the curriculum. As a philosophy of education, service-learning reflects the belief that education must be linked to social responsibility and that the most effective learning is active and connected to experience in some meaningful way (Giles et al. 1991: 7). What makes an experience meaningful differs from individual to individual, but the link between the social significance of an activity and an individual's perception of the value of participating can promote powerful reflective insights.

As a result, service-learning can play an important role in moral development. Human development theorists who have influenced service-learning include Piaget (1932), Kohlberg (1963), and Phenix (1964). Learning activities should be integrated under conditions "where significance is realized" and which "feed moral interests and develop moral insight" (Dewey 1915). In this area as in others, understanding and improved moral problem solving result from reflection.

While a detailed discussion of social foundations and philosophies of education is beyond the scope of this chapter, one theorist seems especially suited to service-learning. Frankenna (1965: 6-10) begins his model of a philosophy of education (Figure 1) with reflection on basic ends or moral principles. Moral considerations start the process, and from this beginning we develop empirical or other premises about human nature and life. From these premises we identify the desired excellences and follow this with research on how to produce them that leads to concrete strategies. The process is continuous and each step logically follows from its predecessor.

Figure 1. Frankenna's Model for a Philosophy of Education (1965)

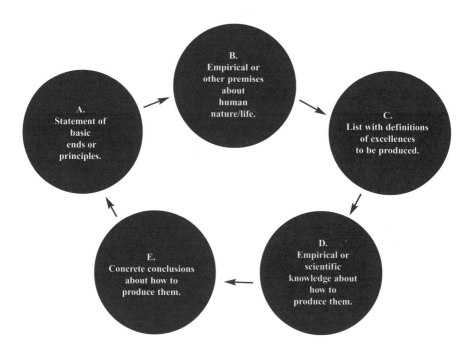

This process, which begins with reflection on our responsibility to the world, seems an appropriate foundation for service-learning in foodservice management. What higher purpose or responsibility could we have than to prepare healthy, tasty, attractive foods served in an appropriate manner? Thus, service-learning implies a program type as well as a philosophy of education. It provides choices among the ways in which students can perform meaningful service in their communities. At the same time, it allows them to improve their technical skills and develop pride in their profession. Strategies for structured reflection contribute to a gradual refinement of the overall process.

New Mexico State's Service-Learning Program

The foodservice group of the Department of Hotel, Restaurant and Tourism Management at New Mexico State University has developed a program for service-learning that uses this model (Figure 2).

Figure 2. Service-Learning Model for Foodservice Management

The initial higher purpose/responsibility module included in Process A is integrated into the mission of and the introduction to the foodservice program in general. Process B has proven to be the most difficult component for students to relate to, and finding activities that improve student technical skills (Process C) has also been a challenge. But the reflection process (D) has always provided ideas that have helped refine the next iteration of the whole.

Each semester, in selected classes, all students are required to complete 16 hours of community service. Originally, service participation received extra credit. However, program evaluations included the complaint that such an arrangement was unfair to those who regularly contributed in class. Furthermore, students not infrequently failed to show up because they regarded the service activity as optional. Two years ago, participation became mandatory and eventually was weighted as 10 percent of the grade.

The service-learning module and experience are introduced on the first day of class. After reviewing the syllabus, the instructor leads a discussion of the responsibilities accepted when embarking on a foodservice career (Process A). The next class session covers the concept of service-learning and includes an introductory exercise. The purpose of this exercise is to provide students with insight into the premise that the recipe for a meaningful life should include service to the community (Process B). Students are formed into groups and view photographs of previous service-learning activities and examples of community-based projects. Students are asked to share at least four examples of this type of activity they have personally experienced in their own lives. Each group is given a large piece of paper and a marker to document the activities on a story board. Story boards from earlier classes are presented as illustrative examples. Fifteen minutes are allotted for this activity, but usually the groups need at least five additional minutes.

Each group then puts up its story board and a discussion ensues. The activities listed include church, school, scouting, choir, band, dance, fraternity, sorority, family, and neighborhood public-service contributions. While some students obviously have been more active, all realize that in their own way they have been connected to the larger community through service. At the end of the class, students are asked to check their Web CT site for comments and are informed that the discussion will continue in the next class.

The following class, a summary of the story boards is distributed along with quotations from former students and a list of service-learning activities for the semester. This list is discussed in detail in the syllabus, where the course value of each activity is also indicated. While certain activities are mandatory, students are allowed to choose among others on the basis of interest. All activities must be documented and evaluated, two by peers or activity sponsors.

Students are responsible for selecting and participating in service activities, and their progress is monitored. To be acceptable, an activity must relate to a student's technical skills improvement (Process C). Sign-up sheets help organize events, and various kinds of guidance are provided. If a student selects an activity and does not appear, the points for that activity and its evaluation are zero — an arrangement that dramatically reduces student absences. The following matrix spells out how each service activity is weighted:

Introductory Exercise	10 points
Service-Learning 4-hour Activity	10 points
Activity Evaluation	10 points
Service-Learning 4-hour Activity	10 points
Peer Activity Evaluation	10 points
Service-Learning 4-hour Activity	10 points
Peer Activity Evaluation	10 points
Service-Learning 4-hour Activity	10 points
Peer Activity Evaluation.	10 points
Closing Exercise and Evaluation	10 points

Grades and progress are listed individually on the Web CT account. A student who is not progressing receives a reminder via email. Students communicate regularly with faculty and peers about their experiences (Process D).

Peer evaluations are probably the most difficult part of the process, but they provide an important connection with other class members. Students are encouraged to document their experiences in a variety of media including videos, photos, and PowerPoint presentations. The closing evaluation is designed to help students share opinions, pictures, PowerPoint, and verbal reports; evaluate the program; and provide suggestions for the next year's activities. Most student responses to the program have been positive, but negative evaluations and comments are usually constructive and relate to the value of an individual activity. Although students are free to choose their experiences, these may not always meet expectations. Ideally, service experiences should provide an impetus for students to continue to contribute to the community throughout their lives. Even more importantly, they should help them develop a framework with which to critically evaluate the types of community service that interest them most.

Meeting Real Community Needs

While service-learning connects students to the hospitality profession and the community, and adds value to the educational process, it also creates ties between the Hotel, Restaurant and Tourism Management program and the community. Some of the program's activities have contributed to the development of funded community outreach projects in a wide range of areas, including inner-city economic development projects, training for low-income youth, and senior-care nutrition programs. Specific service-learning projects have involved serving lunch to the homeless at a soup kitchen and a variety of fundraising events (American Cancer Society, United Way, Alzheimer's Foundation, and festivals too numerous to list). In addition, the integration of service-learning projects into grants from HUD and the USDA has provided an opportunity for students to mentor at risk-students and to focus attention on making the foodservice industry an "industry of choice."

Perhaps most importantly, from the standpoint of this volume, the overall initiative has led students to refine and improve the service-learning process itself (Process E). Certain activities have been discontinued, new ones have been implemented, and students and faculty have developed a better understanding of what kinds of projects merit participation. The program's favorable publicity has given the department a wide range of events to choose from. Publicity has also contributed to the institutionalization of community outreach in the hospitality-education process, earned respect for the department, and helped the program's recruiting efforts. Faculty are beginning to discuss how to reward colleagues involved in these activities with release time, credit toward tenure, and pay raises.

Conclusion

One way or another, foodservice educators are going to "volunteer" and "be volunteered" to serve in a variety of community activities. Moving from volunteerism to service-learning can help create a structure that promotes successful community experiences. The service-learning model and examples discussed above, based on progressive and humanistic principles, may help other educators devise service-learning activities of their own. While structure and organization are certainly vital, the most important component is the reflection that enables students to process their experience. Indeed, it is this reflective component that ultimately makes a service activity into service-learning.

References

American Culinary Federation. (2002). "ACF Charter." www.acfchefs.org/govern/bylaw03.html:1.

Baskette, Michael. (2001). *The Chef Manager.* Saddle River, NJ: Prentice Hall.

Brown, L, Edwin. (Oct. 1982). "The Professional Chef Today, A Report from the Resort Food Executive Conference." *Culinary Review.*

Chef and Child Foundation. (2002). "ACF Chef and Child." www.acfchefs.org/ccf/chefs-giv.html: 1-4.

Clark, Sue Campbell. (2000). "The More We Serve, the More We Learn: Service-Learning in a Human Resource Management Course." *In Working for the Common Good.* Edited by Paul Godfrey and Edward Grasso, 353-373. Washington, DC: AAHE.

Crosby, M. A. (1994). "A History of Helping Hands." *Restaurants USA* 11 (8): 35-38.

Dewey, John. (1915). *Democracy in Education.* New York: Simon & Schuster.

Dornenburg, Andrew, and Karen Page. (1996). *On Becoming a Chef.* Saddle River, NJ: Prentice Hall.

Frankenna, William. (1965). *Philosophy of Education.* New York: McMillan.

Giles, Dwight, Ellen Porter Honnet, and Sally Migliore, eds. (1991). *Research Agenda for Combining Service and Learning in the 1990s.* Raleigh, NC: National Society for Internships and Experiential Education.

Hamesfahr, E.A. (Nov.1934). "Chefs Step Forward." *Culinary Review:* 29.

Hegarty, Joseph. (Winter 1990). "Challenges and Opportunities for Creating Hospitality and Tourism Education Programs in Developing Countries." *Hospitality & Tourism Educator:* 12-13.

Kim, H. Young. (1999). "Giving a Helping Hand to a Hunger Program: Combining Service-Learning and Managerial Communication Basics." *Journal of Hospitality & Tourism Education* 11 (2/3): 22-23.

Kohlberg, Lawrence. (1963). "Moral Development and Identification." In *Child Psychology*. Edited by N.B. Henry and H.G. Richey, 322-323. Chicago: University of Chicago Press.

Johnson, W.H. (Jan./June 1943). "Chicago Public Schools Support the War Effort." *Chicago Schools Journal*: 55.

Lapp, John. (1941). *The Washburne Trade School*. Chicago: Chicago Press.

Mandabach, Keith. (2002). "Lessons from the Depression: American Professional Culinary Arts Programs 1927-1941." *PRAXIS, the Journal of Applied Hospitality Management* 5 (1): 35-52.

Michaelson, L.K., L.D. Fink, and A. Knight. (1996). "What Every Faculty Developer Needs to Know about Learning Groups." In *To Improve the Academy: Resources for Faculty, Instructional and Organizational Development*, 373-397. Stillwater, OK: New Forums Press.

Morrison, Alistair. (1996). *Hospitality and Travel Marketing*. Albany: Del Mar.

O'Halloran, Robert, and Cynthia O'Halloran. (1999). "Service Learning in the Hospitality and Tourism Business Environment." *Journal of Hospitality & Tourism Education* 10 (4): 18-22.

Ornstein, Allan C., and Francis P. Hunkings. (1998). *Curriculum: Foundations, Principles and Issues*. Boston: Allyn & Bacon.

Phenix, Phillip H. (1964). *Realms of Meaning*. New York: McGraw-Hill.

Piaget, Jean. (1932). *The Moral Judgment of a Child*. London: Routledge and Kegan.

Shircliffe, Arnold. (1943). *Principles of Cookery*. Chicago: U.S. Navy.

Sleade, Cheryl. (1998). "Volunteering to Teach Means You Learn Life's Little Lessons." *Hosteur* 8 (3): 19.

Staff. (1933). *L.A. School Journal* 5 (4): 1.

Willy, John Knight, Jr. (Aug. 1942). "Training School Demonstrates Value." *The Hotel Monthly*: 64.

The Secret Ingredient in the New Recipe for Hospitality Education:
Service-Learning as Andragogy

by Joseph Koppel

This chapter will share the secret ingredient that the author has discovered in his practice of service-learning in hospitality education. This ingredient, though especially effective in the hospitality curriculum, would also seem to be transferable to other academic disciplines.

I discovered this ingredient in response to a simple question: Should service-learning be practiced differently in K-12 than in higher education? Educators commonly use the phrase "the pedagogy of service-learning," but is this phrase accurate, or misleading? I suggest we must stop applying this phrase indiscriminately to all levels of education (K-16). If hospitality educators are to be effective, they must make the right choice of teaching methods from a "menu" of assumptions about how their students learn.

In the following pages, I will first present an overview of my service-learning practice at the University of San Francisco (USF). Second, I will divulge the secret ingredient for successful practice from two contrasting sets of learning assumptions. These assumptions constitute *andragogy,* or an adult, student-centered model, and *pedagogy,* a teacher-centered model primarily related to children. Third, I will apply these assumptions to my hospitality service-learning courses. Fourth, I will share some feedback from students and community leaders as well as observations of my own.

An Overview of Service-Learning at USF

Before going to the main course of this paper — the selection of learning assumptions — let's have an appetizer on how I came to get involved in service-learning. A former hospitality colleague once asked me, "Is serving a meal to families at a women's shelter service-learning?" My reply was an emphatic no. While service-learning can be broadly understood, here is how I have come to understand this term. It refers to

> *the academically rigorous process of linking course curricula to student engagement through real-world problems and needs within our communities. This intellectual and civic engagement of students and faculty helps*

institutions of higher learning bring their scholarly resources to bear on the community needs, as well as assists students in experiencing the relevance of classroom instruction. (AAHE 1998)

While serving a meal at a community shelter is an example of kindness, it is not service-learning. Indeed, it is not even a form of experiential learning. The absence of structured reflection (for instance, on why the service is needed) disqualifies it from either. In addition, casual community involvement and a fleeting relationship are — at least ideally — uncharacteristic of service-learning. What was the lasting result of this activity? It is now a little clearer, I hope, why *just* serving a dinner to people in need is not service-learning.

My introduction to service-learning came when a USF colleague, Dr. Susan Prion, asked if I would consider having any of my classes become involved with community organizations, and I replied that I was open to the idea. She gave me USF handouts and readings that captured my attention. Prion (1995) defined service-learning at USF as the "planned, systemic integration of classroom and community to the mutual benefit [of both]." As the then coordinator of service-learning, she provided my classes with an orientation to service-learning as well as a list of community organizations screened for their interest in having students work with them. Initially, the students resisted, primarily because of a lack of time. Some also noted that they were paying many tuition dollars ($15,000 per year) for an education, and they were not in college to help nonprofit organizations. I asked, or more accurately begged, the students to give this new learning-teaching strategy a chance. After all, we were a Jesuit school with a strong commitment to service to the disenfranchised and needy members of our community. I reminded them that, when USF was first opened, the faculty helped educate, among others, the local gold miners. Analogously, our classes were now serving the needy of our contemporary community.

After this introduction, I made a commitment to service-learning and wanted to learn more about it. I was impressed to learn that service-learning has a rich history and is regarded by some as a "revolution in American education." Some of its early and notable supporters included Donald Kennedy (president emeritus of Stanford) and Peter Drucker (management guru, author, and professor at Claremont College). Indeed, one respected educational thinker, Ernest Boyer, the former president of the Carnegie Foundation for the Advancement of Teaching, articulated a new educational vision based on this kind of work:

The new "American College" would celebrate teaching and selectively sup-port research, while also taking pride in the capacity to connect thought to action, theory to practice. . . .Undergraduates at the college participate in field projects relating to real life. Classrooms and laboratories would be extended to include clinics, youth centers, schools and government offices. Faculty members would build partnerships with practitioners who would, in turn, come to the campus as lecturers and student advisers. The New American College, as a connected institution, would be committed to improving, in a very intentional way, the human condition. As clusters of such colleges formed, a new model of excellence in higher education would emerge, one that would enrich the campus, renew communities, and give new dignity and status to the scholarship of service. (Boyer 1994)

As my students and I moved outside the classroom, we really began to get acquainted with our city and its needs. This is when our learning grew rapidly. Students met with leaders from soup kitchens, shelters, AIDS projects, and numerous programs for the homeless, just as Boyer had described for the new American College. Our work began to reflect our commitment to improving the human condition.

The Secret Ingredient: Comparing Child and Adult Learning Assumptions

Hospitality educators can make the best choice from a menu of learning assumptions only if they understand and accept that chil-dren and adults learn differently. Think about this: Do parents and teachers treat an eight-year-old differently than an-18-year-old? Most of us would answer, yes in most situations. This general agreement will guide us in our review of how we teach our students in *higher edu-cation,* which is the focus of this paper. The secret ingredient in our recipe will derive primarily from an "andragogy" model — an adult-learner-centered set of assumptions. Contrasting two very different sets of learning assumptions constitutes our main course.

Generally, we use the term pedagogy to refer to the art and sci-ence of teaching. It is an expert-centered approach. *Pedagogy of the Oppressed* (1973) by Paulo Freire is familiar to many of us, and it was my first introduction to the word. But pedagogy primarily refers to the education of children. In the case of Freire, one could easily, and mistakenly, infer that his followers were children. However, they were not children but, for the most part, impoverished and illiterate adults. It was perhaps their illiteracy, rather than their age, that made their learning similar to that of children.

"Pedagogy" is derived from the Greek words meaning "child" and "leader of." Historically, our approach to teaching evolved between the seventh and twelfth centuries A.D., when children in the monastic and cathedral schools were taught to perform church duties. As secular schools later developed, this teaching method, the sole educational model, was adapted to general teaching practice. In a sense, we have been frozen in a method based on how we teach children, and have applied it to all levels of education — elementary, secondary, and postsecondary. To be sure, there may be times even in higher education when learning assumptions from this model are appropriate to a particular learner or situation. But the choice as to whether a child's or an adult's learning assumptions should be invoked represents a framework decision for educators. Keeping this decision in mind has been helpful to me as a practical guide in designing my own teaching strategies.

Andragogy — defined as "any professionally guided activity that aims at a change in adult persons" — developed primarily in Europe during the last century. It began to be applied in the United States to the training of adults during World War II. Industry and the military needed effective ways to train a shifting work force. Malcolm Knowles pioneered the formal study of this approach. His book, *The Adult Learner: The Definitive Classic in Adult Education and Human Resource Development*, now in its fifth edition, first appeared in 1968 and is being applied both in adult and continuing education and in academic and professional areas, specifically in training and human resource development. Let us look at how the two sets of learning assumptions compare.

Knowles's Learning Assumptions

Pedagogy (child): Teacher-Directed

1. The student needs to know only what is needed to pass.
2. The teacher regards the student as dependent.
3. The student's experience has little value.
4. Readiness happens when the teacher defines what is needed to pass.
5. Learning is subject-centered.
6. The student is motivated by external sources:
   e.g., grades and the teacher's approval.

Andragogy (adult): Student-Centered

1. The student needs to know only why, before undertaking learning.
2. The student has a self-concept of being responsible for decisions.
3. The student is more experienced in life and aware of the community.
4. Readiness to learn derives from a need to cope with real-life situations.
5. Learning is personal: task- or problem-centered.
6. Motivators are internal: e.g., self-esteem and quality of life.

Foremost for the hospitality educator to understand here is that, unlike some restaurant menus, substitutions are allowed! The instructor has two choices of teaching methods for any given situation. In addition, the teacher has numerous choices among the learning assumptions related to the task and the learner: a few from one set, some from the other. It is seldom, if ever, exclusively either-or.

One major difference between the two sets is that in the teacher-directed model the learner's prior experience counts for little. Contrast this with the adult learner's assumption that they are experienced in life and in the community. As many in higher education are aware, significant progress has been made in service-learning in K-12. In California, for example, it is projected that by year 2004, 50 percent of all school districts will have a service-learning requirement on all three levels of instruction. Many of the students who enter higher education in the future will bring valuable service-learning experiences. If this is not accepted, or welcomed, there will be conflict. In other words, experienced students — whether adult or traditional-aged — can more easily develop meaningful service-learning projects than can inexperienced students. College educators must take this circumstance into account in choosing their learning assumptions.

The Andragogy of Hospitality Service-Learning

In accord with Knowles's first assumption concerning andragogy, I would lead a discussion on why we should work with community-based organizations (CBOs). Some students would question the relevance of such work, since they expect to be working for profit-making organizations after graduation. I would respond that opportunities such as internships were already available for working with for-profit business. Furthermore, the university's mission calls for its members to perform service for the common good. In order to be of service, we would need to become aware of how the members of our local community live. In *Pedagogy of the Oppressed*, Freire describes this process as "consciousness-raising."

The second of Knowles's assumptions relates to the learner's self-concept. When I began to accept that my students could be trusted to make some of their own decisions and were capable of self-direction (not an easy task), I became more effective in my service-learning practice. At one time, there were between three and six team projects in my classes. I provided guidelines, minimum requirements, quality standards, and in some cases specific focus areas, such as homeless shelters or soup kitchens (hospitality-related CBOs), but I didn't (and couldn't) micromanage all of this work. However, the primary reason I took this leap of faith was that I had become aware that my higher education students were adults. I had begun to sense that most of them would learn and grow differently than students at lower levels. By treating them like children and making them overly dependent on the classroom, I would actually stunt their growth.

A third learning assumption relates to a learner's prior experience. As I have noted, more and more students in higher education have experienced service in K-12 or through community volunteering. Does this mean they have all become "adults"? While we know that some students graduate, even from college, with little sense of self-direction, perhaps we should ask why this is the case. What real choices have we given them? What reasonable risks have we provided?

A fourth assumption concerns readiness to learn. A part of the transition to adulthood is learning to cope effectively with real-life situations. In every college open house I have attended, either as a parent or more commonly as a faculty member, parents and prospective students have indicated that knowledge and growth are equally important in the higher education experience. Accordingly, hospitality educators also need to be concerned with both. Service-learning has much to offer in both areas. To deliver a good product to a community organization is a real-life challenge. As students become aware of the needs of the community, they grow by creating a product or service to meet those needs.

A fifth learning assumption relates to an orientation to learning. Most students in higher education are motivated to learn when the learning is related to what is happening in their own lives. When educators can demonstrate that the needs of the community should be of concern to all members of the university, this creates a motivation to learn. We need to have everyone's buy-in of the university's mission and its relationship to each person's personal and professional life. When students are invited to identify ways in which they can improve the community, their efforts will result in good service-learning projects.

A final assumption also concerns motivation. While adults are generally responsive to external motivators, such as better job prospects or grades, their major motivators are internal factors like self-esteem and quality of life. Indeed, students are concerned about the impact of the homeless on the quality of life, especially in cities where hospitality/tourism is the leading industry. They also want their efforts to amount to more than simply giving back information on a Scantron sheet. By the end of the semester, many service-learning students are so alive and willing to describe their experiences to classmates that they return to class the following semester to share their service-learning stories. Some also continue working at their CBO. How many students show interest in coming back to talk about the score they got on a conventional final exam?

Hospitality Course Applications

Along with the selection of learning assumptions as our primary ingredients, we need more information for this recipe to be complete. Here I will present some of the projects that two of my hospitality classes developed with the community.

For years I have taught a beverage management/wine tasting course. At first I was perplexed as to how I could integrate a service-learning into this class. Then I happened to read a newspaper article about a "Meal on Wheels Gala Dinner and Wine Auction." I knew the chair of the event, Joyce Goldstein, former owner of one of San Francisco's great restaurants, Square One. We talked, and this opened the door to a possible opportunity. Meeting with students from the class, we discussed what services the organization performed and what meaningful assistance the class might provide. We agreed the students could perform two basic services. First, they could review the meals donated by chefs and pair them with donated wines. This directly applied one of the most complex topics in the beverage course, challenging students to draw upon theories of food and wine pairing. Second, they could serve the wines at the dinner and comment on their flavor components.

Before the event, a representative from the CBO visited the class and showed a video about its program. The students were given a history of Meals on Wheels, an organization that has made an immeasurable difference in the lives of homebound senior citizens and has provided more than five million meals over the last 26 years. Thus, the beverage service-learning project added value to the class in several ways, even as the class added value to the event. We learned so much more that evening than is possible in a typical beverage service class. Other beverage classes did similar projects, in which the students worked with some of the greatest chefs and winemakers in the nation.

My Introduction to Hospitality class undertook a different kind of project. These first-year students seemed so young that I was unsure if they were able to do a service-learning project. However, as a member of the board of directors of the Haight Ashbury Food Program, I was involved with new foodservice job-training programs for the homeless, and this offered an opportunity. I divided the class into three teams and assigned each a job-training program. One of the course readings was Bill Shore's *Revolution of the Heart* (1995). With this book, we laid a foundation for our service-learning efforts. As some readers may already know, Shore created what is probably the largest foodservice fund-raising program, Taste of a Nation, an annual food and wine tasting event held across the country. Local CBOs can apply to the national organization in Washington, DC, for funds raised by the program.

One of the book's most important passages, for our purposes, is a statement by M.F.K. Fisher, considered by many to be one of the greatest literary writers on food:

> It seems to me that our three basic needs, for food and security and love, are so mixed and mingled and entwined that we cannot straightly think of one without the other. So it happens that when I write of hunger, I am really writing about love and the hunger for it, and then warmth and the love of it and the hunger for it . . . and then the warmth and the richness and fine reality of hunger satisfied . . . and it is all one. There is a communion of more than our bodies when bread is broken and wine is drunk. And that is my answer when people ask me: Why do you write about hunger, and not wars or love?

As this class evolved, I too felt at times like a new student, learning to facilitate student inquiry rather than serving as the teacher-expert with all the answers. As a group, we began to better understand the connections among food, security, and caring, as well as important things about our community. With a new sense of commitment, we began to apply technical references in our hospitality textbook, reviewing some of the principles of food operations and sanitation. The students did a literature search to find guidelines for training programs. Armed with this course material, they were able to set out as hospitality "consultants" to the three programs. They could meet with the instructors and their students to determine other resource needs, and could also plan an end-of-semester celebration and "graduation" party for all participants.

In both of these hospitality service-learning courses, we were able to apply theory to practice, and discovered we could develop a meaningful result. We learned we could make a difference through our professional skills. And our deeper awareness of some often-overlooked members of the community made us better citizens.

Useful Procedures

In the process of overseeing these projects, I discovered several useful resources. The first was the Community Interest Form. This helped our community partners better understand the students' interests, skills and knowledge, transportation issues, and time availability. Another form was the Service Agreement, in which the student team and community defined the performance specifics of a project. Also useful in this regard was an attendance record.

Another important set of resources related to reflection. In my beverage classes, we recorded our organoleptic (total senses) impressions of the wines, but this was just the beginning. Drawing upon the work of Dick Cone at the University of Southern California, I developed the evaluation-reflection component in the courses with the help of a handout entitled "Ethics and Service Learning." Early in the course, I set the stage for this component by asking how many students felt it was better to give than to receive. Usually most hands would go up. Then I explained how the students were probably going to experience something new in their service-learning work. That work would rest on three principles fundamental to ethical practice:

• Reciprocity. All participants in the service-learning equation should both give and receive. There should be true equality among the students, faculty, and community partners. This implied joint planning, joint responsibilities, and joint evaluation. A team report would be considered incomplete if all it reported was what the students gave to the project.

• Quality. Performance specifications for the project should be meaningful and relevant. This required attention to detail, clear lines of communication, active problem solving, and collaborative work.

• Reflection. All participants should note their personal reactions to the project. Keeping a journal of their experiences and reactions was one popular way to achieve this goal.

Feedback from Students, Faculty, and Community Leaders

It is now time for dessert, a final course intended to round off the story. In the context of the following remarks, consider the question: What would the learning outcomes have been if these courses had been based on a traditional, teacher-centered pedagogy?

Here is one representative student comment:

> So many times businesses tend to overlook the social obligation that is created by their success. When one is successful . . . it is necessary to give back to the community in order to maintain an equilibrium mindset that diverges from the sometimes selfish nature of success. . . . I will never forget the lessons that I learned in our group project working with the Food Runners organization. In our classes we learned the skills of a leader and how to facilitate the creation of an efficient work environment. We also learned how to take these skills and apply them to the real world, but not the usual business internship, this was an experience with a higher cause. We took our skills and we learned to help others in need by helping make Food Runners a more efficient organization. . . . Food Runners allowed me to see both sides of our competitive society. I saw the people who ate in the fancy restaurants and had no concerns about where their next meal coming from. And then when I delivered the food I saw those who had so little that the food I brought was enough to give meaning to their day. This project heightens my social awareness as well as teaching me to take the knowledge that I have been blessed with in the classroom and help others with it.

Another student contributed this view from the introductory hospitality class:

> There is always a danger that when you view people only as members of a group and not as individuals that you strip them of their dignity in the process. I know I previously thought of the homeless more as some kind of monolithic unsolvable problem than as individuals with unique and varied characteristics, in short, dehumanizing them. However, it is difficult to think that way of people after you have actually shared an experience together with them. It might not have been a great amount of time, but it was enough to make both the program and the individuals real to me. In a sense, we are still participating in the program as we write about it, talk about it with our friends or even think about it.

Here is another student from the same class:

> The goals of Share Our Strength are being mirrored in the work of these foodservice job-training programs. People need skills to change their lives more than they need a handout. For that reason these programs are critical to eradicating poverty, according to Bill Shore. As is noted, a new phi-

losophy is needed, not the same old polarity of politics between the Republicans and Democrats.

One of the community partners, the event chair and executive director of Meals on Wheels, wrote:

> Thank you so much for generously donating your time and expertise in our Gala Dinner and Wine Auction. We also want to acknowledge and thank the students from your beverage management class. They were wonderful and worked really hard throughout the dinner. We think it wonderful how you are able to involve your class at fundraising events for organizations such as ours. We hope that by making this experience an extension of the classroom your students are able to gain knowledge about wine and beverage service and at the same time make a contribution to the community.

And finally, here is what one of the leaders of the Haight Ashbury Food Program wrote:

> I was very impressed with the student's energy and enthusiasm for the project. It made me glad to see so-called "Generation X-ers" interested in compassionate service. Moreover, their professionalism was much greater than what I would have expected from college students. I also think the educational process involved in working with the Food Program was much greater than just the written production of written material for us, and I commend you and the University for encouraging education of this nature.

As the faculty partner, I can summarize what the projects have meant to me: They have occasioned an academic rebirth. I have come to realize just how many choices educators have in how they teach their discipline. No longer do we have to rely only on traditional, teacher-centered methods. While we still need the theories communicated in lectures and textbooks, we also have the ability to achieve other important learning outcomes. However, those outcomes require that we stop regarding our students as children who need to be force-fed.

Conclusion

I am reminded of a familiar saying from the kitchen: "The proof is in the pudding." This culinary axiom refers to how we test the quality of custard. If a knife is inserted and comes out clean, the dessert is deemed acceptable. The proof of the effectiveness of service-learning in hospitality education can be found in the evaluations of participants. One testimony in particular stands out in my mind. As a particular student team made its final semester report, it seemed to me unlike any other in my 20-plus years of university teaching. The team reported that their service-learning experience had taught them a new meaning for the term Darwinism. I was perplexed by this comment, until they reported to the class that, as a result of their service-learning experience, they had discovered that "the fittest must help others to survive." They conveyed, through that statement, that they had experienced knowledge, comprehension, application analysis, synthesis, and evaluation in reaching their conclusion — Bloom's entire Cognitive Taxonomy. How could I, by myself, ever teach a class in which students achieved such a complex learning outcome? These service-learning experiences helped me better understand the wisdom of Confucius' "Good teaching is never forgotten."

Everyone knows that medical practice treats children and adults differently. Why shouldn't education? Let hospitality management lead the way in developing learning strategies appropriate for the adult students with whom we work. Make no mistake: It will be difficult to let go of my teacher-expert role. But it can also feel good to do so. Let us begin selecting, from a complete menu, those teaching and learning strategies that best fit our students and their developmental needs. Let us begin to accept and practice the *andragogy* of service-learning.

References

American Association for Higher Education. (1998). www.aahe.org.

Boyer, E. (March 9, 1994). "Creating the New American College." *The Chronicle of Higher Education*: A48.

Freire, Paulo. (1973). *Pedagogy of the Oppressed*. New York: The Seabury Press.

Knowles, Malcolm S. (1998). *The Adult Learner: The Definitive Classic in Adult Education and Human Resource Development*. 5th edition. Woburn, MA: Butterworth-Heinmann.

Prion, Susan. (1995). University of San Francisco service-learning handout.

Shore, Bill. (1995). *Revolution of the Heart: A New Strategy for Creating Wealth and Meaningful Change*. New York: Riverhead Books.

Enhancing the Hospitality Curriculum with Service-Learning

by Vern Markey and Pamela Holsinger-Fuchs

College students have a lot to offer their community. They have writing, artistic, problem-solving, and organizational skills. These can make a big difference to an organization or project struggling to improve the environment or the lives of people. Knowledge that students gain through academic courses can be put to use while they are still in school (Bringle and Hatcher 1996).

Service-learning is a pedagogy that allows students to gain a better understanding of academic content by applying their skills and knowledge to benefit society. When they work on projects with local residents and leaders, they can learn as they serve their communities. They are exposed to issues such as economics, demographics, state and local political systems, and environmental resource management.

Service-Learning Pedagogy

Service-learning in the hospitality curriculum enhances personal and professional development and encourages a sense of community responsibility. Students sharpen their communication skills and increase their knowledge of how organizations function within the community (Stevens 1997/1998). The resources that universities possess become accessible to the community when service-learning addresses community issues and needs (Bringle and Hatcher 1996).

Many college programs offer students field experience through internships, practica, and residencies, but these experiences are designed to achieve learner outcomes without focusing on a sense of community and civic responsibility. Furthermore, service opportunities to the larger community are not often connected to the curriculum (Hayes Godar 2000). Incorporating service-learning into curricula sharpens the students' skills while enabling the community to experiences economic and social benefits (Bringle and Hatcher 1996).

The service-learning instructional methodology integrates community service with academic instruction as it focuses on reflective thinking and civic responsibility. Service-learning programs involve students in organized community service that addresses local needs while developing their academic skills, sense of civic responsibility, and commitment to the community. Service-learning does not include cooperative education, practica, or internship programs but can serve as training leading up to these experiences. In other words, service-learning expands the four walls of the classroom and gives students hands-on learning experiences while they help others.

Faculty support and involvement are crucial for successful service-learning. Since service-learning must be a course-driven feature of the curriculum if it is to become meaningful, students must see the value of it (Bringle and Hatcher 1996), and faculty must ensure the experience is valuable for each of the stakeholders involved: faculty, students, administration, and community organizations.

Markus, Howard, and King (1993) collected data from evaluations in courses using service-learning experiences. Their findings showed significant differences between groups that completed service-learning projects and those that completed only traditional requirements. Students completing service-learning said that they performed up to their potential in the courses and that they learned to apply principles from their coursework to varying situations. Interestingly, the authors also found a higher rate of attendance in class sections using service-learning compared to those that did not. Many students are now looking for faculty who incorporate service as part of the curriculum, "not just from books and lectures" (Eyler and Giles 1999).

Some advantages that service-learning offers in the hospitality curriculum are:

• It helps the institution foster caring, personal interactions among students, faculty, and community.

• It helps institutions meet their need for partnerships and collaborations.

• It helps build the relationship between the institution and the community.

• It is a medium through which the community and students can receive first-hand experience of each other.

• It satisfies core components, such as active learning and teamwork.

• It applies knowledge, which is good for the students.

• It provides a project method of teaching (a broader definition of laboratory).

• It brings high-tech and high-touch together.

• It integrates communication skills.

In hospitality programs, our aim should be twofold: to educate managers and encourage a responsible citizenry (DeFranco and Abbott 1996).

Service-Learning in Hospitality Management

Service-learning projects in the hospitality curriculum can be creative and reach far into the community. A typical project might include students helping out at the local soup kitchen. However, there are many less obvious opportunities that can be used in undergraduate courses.

One of the authors, while an instructor in the Hotel, Restaurant, and Institutional Management (HRI) program at the University of Minnesota, Crookston (UMC), used service-learning in several upper-level undergraduate courses, including Institutional Food Service Administration and Global Tourism. Students enrolled in the foodservice administration class in spring 1998 and 1999 were given group projects; students enrolled in the tourism course in fall 1998, 1999, and 2000 completed service-learning projects individually.

The First Menu Project. The first foodservice administration group was given the task of developing a cyclical menu for a nonprofit, long-term care facility located in a small town. The facility serves three meals per day plus an evening snack to approximately 80 patients. The project included development of a comprehensive menu plan that followed guidelines set forth by the Omnibus Budget Reconciliation Act of 1987 (OBRA). The OBRA guidelines require nutritionally balanced meal plans with accommodations for special need options, such as pureed or vegetarian. All of the menu items needed to be nutritionally balanced and pre-costed to determine the feasibility of offering them on the menu. The facility administrator provided guidelines for maximum daily expenditures for each patient ($3.75 per patient per day). In addition, menus were to reflect special dietary needs such as low cholesterol or low sodium.

The facility does not have a registered dietician on staff. However, the students in the class were all preparing to be dietetic technicians and were able to consult with both the instructor and a registered dietician throughout the project. The class visited the site at the onset of its work, to determine patient needs as well as which type of menu items were most appropriate, given preparation requirements, equipment availability, and staff expertise.

By the end of the term, the students had completed the project and submitted a final report with recommendations (for example, the facility should consider purchasing some products in smaller quantities to free up storeroom space). The report also included a two-week revolving menu consisting of recipes, cost information, and a purchasing guide for special dietary needs. All menu days remained within the $3.75 daily maximum.

At the completion of the project, the students were asked for comments. These indicated that many of the group thought the task very time-consuming but regarded their efforts worthwhile. Having had an opportunity to see the facility and, in some cases, visit with patients, they found the project very rewarding. They had used skills that are often difficult to design and assess in classroom-based projects. They were able to demonstrate competencies such as problem solving, communication, and teamwork. (Some of their reflections are included in the discussion section of this paper.)

A second group project was similar to the first, except that the facility was a homeless shelter. The class visited the site to assess its needs, analyze its space and equipment, and determine food-product availability and staff expertise. The assignment was to develop a two-week cyclical menu that included breakfast, lunch, and dinner. The greatest challenge was the limited variety of food products, since the facility relies on government subsidies and private donations, and some choices, such as fresh fruits or vegetables, were not always available. The task became how to identify menu items and recipes that were both nutritious and cost-effective. In addition, because of limitations related to budget, equipment availability, and staff expertise, the menus and recipes needed to be simple to prepare.

The result of this group's efforts was a two-week cyclical menu whose recipes could be adjusted according to food availability. The students demonstrated problem solving, communication, and teamwork skills. (Comments from this group are also included in the discussion section of this paper.)

The Tourism Project. The Global Tourism course is designed to explore the various groups that make up the travel and tourism industry. These include the hotel and restaurant industries, the airlines and other modes of transportation, leisure, gaming, cruise ships, and entertainment. Students in this course complete projects, assignments, and exams that require readings from the text, additional readings placed on reserve in the college library, and materials from the Internet.

In fall 1998, four of the students in the class elected to complete a service-learning project, while the others chose to complete a research paper. Those electing the service-learning project had the option of developing their own project or choosing from projects already identified. The instructor had arranged with local organizations to assess their interest in this project and to brainstorm ideas. Some ideas required more students than were available, and had to be rejected. Those students who chose to develop their own projects received simple guidelines: Identify a real-world situation in which you can use and develop skills in organizing, problem solving, and communications while providing a service to an organization that wants help.

Of the four students who opted for the service-learning project, two chose instructor ideas and two others found their own projects. Of the two students who selected instructor ideas, one worked with the Minnesota Extension Office on the UMC campus to plan and organize a conference, a project that helped the student clarify career choices. The student had been planning a career in conference and convention planning, but after this project decided to pursue other areas within the hospitality industry. A second student chose to work on a project with the local Chamber of Commerce. Of the two students who developed their own projects, one planned a student trip for the UMC Multicultural Club to Winnipeg, Manitoba. The other planned a trip for the UMC Choir to London and Paris.

Since student evaluations indicated that the service projects were enjoyable and contributed substantially to the learning process, the instructor decided that in the future all students would complete service-learning projects and would not have the option of writing a research paper instead. Thus, in fall 1999 and 2000, the students enrolled in Global Tourism were required to complete a service-learning project as one of the course requirements. Options included working with the local Chamber of Commerce, a regional snowmobile club, a travel and tourist information center, or the student-activities office on campus. Each student worked with an organizational staff member who acted as site supervisor. The site supervisor was asked to track the student's progress and was expected to provide feedback to the student and instructor.

The feedback from project supervisors was formative as well as summative. The formative feedback, although informal, was used to ensure that each student was making progress and not waiting until the last week or two of the term to complete the course requirements. The summative feedback was in the form of an evaluation sheet completed by the site supervisor (Figure 1). In addition, each student was asked to complete an activity report (Figure 2) and was required to prepare and present the project to the class. To assign a score for the project, the instructor used the formative and summative evaluations as well as the student presentation. The project score contributed to the student's overall score and final letter grade for the course.

Figure 1. Student Volunteer Assessment Form
(Completed by Site Supervisor)

Directions for Students — Please complete all requested information in the box only.

Name_____ Date_____

Community Partner_____

Address_____

Supervisor_____ Date of Service: from __ ____ to _ _____

Supervisor's Title_____

Supervisor's Telephone Number_____

Directions: Supervisor, please circle which number best rates this student's performance in terms of the following qualities.

	Excellent	Good	Satisfactory	Fair	Poor
Ability to work with minimal supervision	5	4	3	2	1
Attendance	5	4	3	2	1
Follows directions	5	4	3	2	1
Punctuality	5	4	3	2	1
Quality of work	5	4	3	2	1
Relationship with co-workers	5	4	3	2	1
Sense of responsibility	5	4	3	2	1
Shows interest	5	4	3	2	1
Uses good judgment	5	4	3	2	1
Willingness to learn	5	4	3	2	1
Overall rating	5	4	3	2	1

Supervisor's comments:

Supervisor's signature:_____ Date:_____

Please return this form to: _____

The service-learning project requirements had by now become very detailed. Students met with the organization contact person (supervisor) to develop a simple plan. The plan included time lines, deadlines, and outcomes. Students were required to keep a journal of their activities, hours spent on assignments and tasks, and personal reflections. This enhanced the reflection dimension of the service-learning, allowing integration of curricular ideas into real-life situations. The students' reflections addressed what they liked and disliked about the project and assignments and whether the goals and outcomes had been met. The instructor collected the journals at intervals to ensure that students were keeping them up. At the end of the project, the students completed an activity report that also included evaluation responses (Figure 2).

Figure 2. Service-Learning Activity Report (Completed by Student)

Name_____

Report period: from_____ to_____

Organization/community name_____

Address_____ Phone number _____

What was your most significant accomplishment this past month/days of service? Comment on its importance.

Looking back on your service activities, what were the high and low points?

What was your most rewarding experience during your time of service? Why?

Explain one thing you did that you would do differently if you had to do it again.

Finish the sentence: "Service-learning for me was . . ."

If any unusual events occurred during your service activities, attach a description of the event(s) to this report.

Additional comments or requests. Attach additional sheets if necessary.

Signed _____
Date   _____

Discussion

The instructor and the students easily located service-learning projects. A wealth of opportunity is waiting at community, college and university, and nonprofit organizations for the hospitality management student who wants to be involved. Students can bring new enthusiasm to such organizations while learning valuable life skills.

Evaluations from students at the end of the term revealed that academic learning had benefited from the service experiences, and participants in the community expressed satisfaction about the help they received and the experience of working with young, energetic people. One student remarked, "I was nervous at first about working with strangers, but soon found the work to be a nice change. Plus I got to show off my skills learned in the classroom." Another wrote, "Providing help to organizations that really need it was rewarding." A third said, "I had an opportunity to meet a lot of people." A service-learning partner wrote that the student "did a lot of work and took the project very seriously. While the student did experience some frustrations, everything went very well." Although some students contributed more effort than others, community partner evaluations were generally "Good" to "Excellent" (Figure 1). A few comments did indicate some student frustration, an example being, "The person I worked with was sometimes difficult to get hold of and she seemed to give me tasks that she simply didn't want to deal with herself."

No statistical analysis of these findings was undertaken, but the students enjoyed their service-learning experiences and scored better on their projects compared to previous years when research papers were assigned. Clearly, the combination of classroom instruction and community service can enhance learning.

References

Bringle, R.G., and J.A. Hatcher. (1996). "Implementing Service-Learning in Higher Education." *Journal of Higher Education* 67 (2): 221-239.

DeFranco, A.L., and J.L. Abbott. (1996). "Teaching Community Service and the Importance of Citizenry." *Hospitality & Tourism Educator* 8 (1): 5-7.

Eyler, Janet, and Dwight Giles. (1999). *Where's the Learning in Service-Learning?* San Francisco: Jossey-Bass.

Hayes Godar, S. (2000). "Live Cases: Service-Learning Consulting Projects in Business Courses." *Michigan Journal of Community Service-Learning* 7: 126-132.

Markus, G.B., J.P. Howard, and D.C. King. (1993). "Integrating Community Service and Classroom Instruction Enhances Learning: Results from an Experiment." *Educational Evaluation and Policy Analysis* 15 (4): 410-419.

Stevens, B. (1997/1998). "Service-Learning: Merging Hospitality and Volunteerism." *Journal of Hospitality & Tourism Education* 9 (4): 63-65.

Transforming Students and Communities Through Service-Learning

by Tom Van Dyke

According to the United States Department of Agriculture, 31 million people live in households that experience hunger or the risk of hunger. This represents 1 in 10 people in the United States (U.S. Department of Agriculture 1999). A report by the U.S. Conference of Mayors in 2001 stated that hunger and homelessness had risen sharply in major cities during the past year. Requests for emergency food assistance had climbed an average of 23 percent, and requests for emergency shelter assistance an average of 13 percent in 26 major cities surveyed (U.S. Conference of Mayors 2001). Hunger and homelessness are just two of the many problems facing people today, as societal problems continue to grow in complexity and scope.

In the search for solutions to the problems facing our society and youth, the role of education is often discussed. What is education's role in solving societal problems? Specifically, do hospitality educators have a responsibility to teach students how to be good citizens? Should our students be concerned about the welfare of the local community and of their future employees?

For the past 12 years, I have been teaching a course, Housing the Homeless and Feeding the Poor, that was originally offered only to hotel/restaurant majors at the University of South Carolina but is now open to any major at Indiana University of Pennsylvania. More than 300 students have been involved in this course and have served approximately 10,500 hours in the community. The course has been challenging and demanding, as well as rewarding. I see students transformed from indifferent or passive recipients of knowledge to active problem-solvers and learners concerned with the welfare of the less fortunate in the community. Students have developed and implemented a food recovery program that sends leftover food from restaurants to local shelters; taught life skills at an abused and battered women's shelter; taught children from the shelter to make nutritious after-school snacks; developed a program for people to donate used cars for individuals in transition from welfare to work; planned and executed fundraising dinners for local shelters; held end-of-semester clothing and food drives for students to donate items they did not want to take home; and raised money for the homeless in Indiana County through a benefit concert. This list identifies only a few of the accomplishments. Furthermore, the fruit of our labor has been the empowerment of students, who saw they could take a real-world problem and contribute to its solution.

Five key elements facilitate student transformation. The first four elements are the specified course requirements: (1) serve 35 hours in the community during the semester, (2) make a presentation on one aspect of hunger or homelessness, (3) write letters to elected officials on relevant pending legislation, and (4) create a semantic network. The fifth and last element involves inviting guest speakers to visit the class and talk about hunger and homelessness in the community.

The Service Project

The course description states that students are required to work 35 hours in the community during the semester (Element 1). To establish a network of service sites, I meet individually with directors of community service agencies (community action programs, adult literacy programs, food banks, Head Start, domestic violence shelters). I explain to the directors that I am teaching a course on housing the homeless and feeding the poor and would like to list their agency in my syllabus as a potential service site. A clear set of expectations, including an agreement that students be involved in meaningful work, is shared with agency directors. Simply answering phones or filing papers will not fulfill the requirement; students should work with agency clients. Additionally, the projects that students complete should add value to existing projects or should fill needs that are beyond the agency's ordinary schedule or budget. Agencies that can ensure this type of opportunity are added to the list of potential service sites in the course syllabus.

On the first day of class, I distribute the syllabus and ask the students to think about the organization with which they would like to work. Students can also consider organizations other than those listed in the syllabus. They then develop groups based on the service site chosen. I am available to answer questions about the various organizations. After the students have decided on an organization, I schedule a time for the student groups to meet with the contact person, who explains the purpose of the organization and the task at hand. The students, the contact person, and I then formulate reasonable goals to be accomplished over the semester. The 35 hours can be spent at the organization or working on a group project for the organization. The resulting contract clearly states what the students plan to accomplish, what the organization will provide, and when and where the students will do their work. The university does not provide transportation, so the students choose projects close to campus or carpool with classmates.

Students are required to keep a daily log in which they can reflect on the service they are providing, voice frustrations or note problems encountered, and think about how this experience relates to information covered in class. The logs are read and returned with notes of encouragement. Students are also instructed to talk to me about problems at a site or with fellow classmates. This is the real world, and problems will arise. Addressing those problems will help the group have a positive service experience. My hope is that the students will become involved in lifelong service, so it is essential that they have positive experiences and that I adjust their expectations if major problems arise. On occasion, efforts to complete a project may fail, thwarted by a last-minute change or cancellation, but these negative experiences can have positive learning consequences. For example, after a family service agency cancelled the project a week prior to an event, the students found another similar event and asked to be included. The students had to adjust their plans, but at least they had a venue for their project. Agencies that don't fulfill their obligations are generally removed from the master list.

Students are also required to submit a group project proposal (Attachment A). Class time is allotted to discuss the projects and any problems the students are experiencing. The class brainstorms to determine how we can improve the projects. For their final exam, groups present their accomplishments, problems encountered, and recommendations to improve their projects. Each writes a project summary for the next group of students that may work on the same project. The presentations are more than just a method for me to measure their success — they mark a time to celebrate what students have accomplished and to reflect on how they might continue their community work. Students proudly tell stories about how they made a difference. They also share visions for the future.

Group Research and Presentation

Element 2 is the students' research on an aspect of hunger or homelessness. As a starting point, the students receive a list of topics and resources from which to choose (Attachment B), each with a packet of information from past class presentations and other information I have collected. After they have completed their research, students present information that concentrates on solutions to the problem, and list organizations (websites) that are attempting to solve it. Both the research and the presentations are done in groups of no more than four individuals. The presentations last no longer than 20 to 30 minutes, with a group-led discussion for an additional 30 minutes.

A week prior to its presentation, each group gives classmates a handout briefly discussing its topic in order to stimulate thought. Another handout, distributed during the presentation, contains references and a brief description of relevant organizations and how they can be accessed. Classmates critique the presentations, citing especially good ideas and effective delivery, expressing their own feelings about the material, and offering suggestions for improvement. I compile the comments and share them with the presenters. The group presentations have been remarkable. Students become advocates for a cause. They learn that while societal iniquities are staggering, social justice is attainable with effective individuals and organizations.

Advocacy

Moving from direct and indirect service to advocacy, individuals write letters to elected officials (Element 3). Each student writes one letter and asks nine other individuals to write letters to legislators about pending legislation or budget considerations for the coming fiscal year. A fact sheet about the issue in question often helps the writers construct more effective letters, which must be typed or handwritten; form letters are never sent. I encourage students to visit the Bread for the World website, where they can find the names and addresses of their U.S. Senators and Representatives. In class, students learn about pending state and federal legislation and are encouraged to explore the variety of websites in the syllabus. They are cautioned about the time-sensitive nature of legislation and budget issues, and are warned they will not receive credit for letters sent after the budget or legislation has been voted on. Students not already registered to vote are encouraged to submit a voter registration form.

In this assignment, the students thus become advocates for the homeless and hungry, who are seldom politically engaged and cannot lobby effectively for legislation that would benefit them. Many students also begin to understand why citizens are apathetic or frustrated. This is the most challenging assignment, and some students do not want to write letters and find it hard to recruit friends or family to write letters. I offer the option of writing a research paper but strongly discourage it.

The Semantic Network

Since there are no tests in this course, the students are required to construct a semantic network (Element 4) and attach a one-page response to the following questions:

• Which ideas presented or discussed in class do you believe can end the hunger and homelessness problem?

• Do you believe the hunger and homeless problem can be reduced significantly?

- What can you do after graduation to promote social justice?

The purpose of the semantic network is for the student to think about how the material in class relates to the objectives of the course.

Semantic networks consist of conceptual nodes and links or statements of relationships connecting them. For those studying and analyzing new content in order to make sense out of it, semantic networks provide rich visual tools for depicting the structure of ideas in a given domain. Learners who build semantic networks are actively seeking important ideas from information sources that they need in order to construct their nets. They are evaluating information for its relevance and the ways it fits together. They are also constructing visual-verbal representations of their own ideas. In this way, they are using an intentional strategy for studying course content. This process requires students to reflect on what they know and how new ideas relate to what they know (Jonassen et al. 1999).

Students are instructed to do the initial design alone and are later given a chance to compare designs. They are also told that there is no one way to complete the project. I look for creativity, how the ideas interconnect with the big picture, and a clear representation of what is important. The assignment can be presented on 8.5 by 11 inch paper or on posterboard, and is evaluated based on thoroughness of content and substance.

Guest Speakers

Guest speakers (Element 5) are the "guiding lights" of the class and the real heroes and heroines of the community. Most of them work for small salaries and experience the constant frustration of stretching an organization's limited resources to meet community needs. They are the role models the students need to see, people in service who exhibit compassion, selflessness, and a determination to make a difference. Four speakers are invited each semester to give the students a basic understanding of the local community.

The first speaker is always the director of a local faith-based homeless shelter. The shelter is only for single adult males and females, and houses mentally and physically disabled and homeless individuals. The director is warm, compassionate, and genuinely cares about the residents. He captivates the students with stories of the variety of people who stay at the shelter and his creativity and ingenuity in raising funds to keep the shelter open.

The next speaker, the homeless liaison coordinator for Armstrong and Indiana counties, talks about homeless children in our rural community and illustrates the grinding poverty some children face. She concludes the presentation by reading "The Day in the Life of a

Homeless Child," which vividly illustrates the hardship faced at school by homeless children. The conclusion is always very moving.

I also invite the director of the local community action program. She discusses the wide variety of programs available to local residents in the community (food bank, energy assistance, family homeless shelter, financial counseling, mortgage assistance program, supported work program, and transportation assistance).

The last person I invite to speak is the director of the Indiana County Assistance Office, which is responsible for administering Temporary Assistance for Needy Families (formerly known as welfare), food stamps, the medical assistance program, and the low-income home-energy-assistance program. Before the director arrives, I remind the students that this office is often caught in the crossfire of politicians' scorn for the programs (which the legislators themselves created), the bureaucracy needed to run the program, and the needy it is supposed to help. The media sometimes look for sensational stories to highlight the corruption and inefficiencies of the programs administered by this office. I want students to hear what this agency does without distortion.

On the first day of class, students receive a list of potential speakers and choose which they would like to hear in class (Attachment C). These speakers are in addition to the four previously mentioned. The students record their options on bubble sheets, which are then scanned and tabulated. The speakers with the highest scores are invited to class and are scheduled for the first part of the semester. Their presentations give the students an understanding of the services provided in our community. Students are required to submit one-page summaries and reflections on each presentation.

Coursework exceeds the typical work level for students; however, at the end of the semester the students have an indelible understanding of the needs of the less fortunate in our community. The class is a win-win situation for all involved. The community service organization receives young, energetic students committed to working on projects deemed important. The university benefits from the goodwill created by the students. The students win by being able to apply their critical thinking and problem-solving skills, and through improved self-esteem gained from applying academic study to real community needs. I benefit by a renewed faith in the students' ability to create a better world. Education does have a role in solving society's problems. If we can develop students committed to working and advocating for the less fortunate in our community, we will have developed citizens.

Attachment A. Group Project Proposal Form (Student Proposal)

LS 499 Housing the Homeless and Feeding the Poor

Extent to which this issue is a problem (provide background information):

Description of proposed project:

What is the timeline of events for this project to be successful?

In what way will this project positively impact the community?

Possible partners (in school and out):

Adapted from the Community Service-Learning Institute at Slippery Rock University of Pennsylvania.

Attachment B. List of Topics

How can citizens change the government to be more responsive to the less fortunate in our society? *The Essential Gandhi, How to Overthrow the Government, Soul of A Citizen, Amazing Grace,* www.democracymatters.org, www.results.org, www.fairvote.org , www.MoveOn.org, www.democracymatters.org, www.rock-thevote.org

How can the homeless be empowered to change their lives? *Each One Teach One (Up and Out of Poverty: Memoirs of a Street Activist), Tell Them Who I Am, Have a Great One!,* www.nationalhomeless.org, www.endhomelessness.org, www.melvilletrust.org, www.csh.org, www.naeh.org.

Government and society have neglected the mentally ill. What should be done about the current crisis? *Mad in America; Out of Bedlam: The Truth about Deinstitutionalization; Out of the Shadows: Confronting America's Mental Illness Crisis,* www.nmha.org, www.nami.org, www.psychlaws.org, www.madnation.cc, www.bazelon.org.

Can American workers survive on minimum wage and no insurance? *The End of Work, Fast Food Nation, Nickled and Dimed,* www.conversion.org, www.communitychange.org, www.thirdsector.co.uk, http://acorn.org, www.npa-us.org.

Poverty has devastating effects on the mental and physical development of children. How can poverty be eliminated? *Common Purpose: Strengthening Families and Neighborhoods to Rebuild America; Within Our Reach; Savage Inequalities: Children in America's Schools*, www.childrensdefense.org, www.stand.org, www.yes.org.

The federal government is decreasing funding for social programs, and nonprofit organizations are trying to fill the gap. How can nonprofits succeed? *Revolution of the Heart, The Cathedral Within, No More Throw-Away People*, www.communitywealth.org, www.timedollar.org, www.strength.org, www.workingforchange.org, www.makeadifferenceday.com.

The corporate hunt for mega-profits has resulted in increased lobbying. Can money buy legislative influence? *The Silent Takeover, Wealth and Democracy, Unequal Protection, The Best Democracy Money Can Buy, When Corporations Rule the World, Corporate Predators, The Post Corporate World, The Divine Right of Capital*, www.socialinvest.org, www.sweatshops.org, www.greenpages.org , www.globalexchange.org, www.business-ethics.com.

Is the current agriculture system tragically flawed? *Diet for a Small Planet, Hope's Edge, The Food Revolution, A Future with Hope, Hunger 2002, Agriculture in the Global Economy, Alternative to Economic Globalization*, www.secondharvest.org, www.bread.org, www.foodfirstfirst.org, www.heifer.org.

Why are we building more prisons? Do prisons neglect rehabilitation? Is government creating a permanent criminal class? *The Rich Get Richer, The Poor Get Prison; The Perpetual Prisoner Machine; The Mythology of Crime & Criminal Justice*, http://ncia.igc.org, www.sentencingproject.org, www.lionheart.org, www.prisonsmart.org.

The United States has a $6 trillion deficit. Last year 26 percent of the federal revenue paid off interest on the national debt. Where should our tax dollars go? *The Soul of Politics, Just Generosity*, www.natprior.org, www.citizen.org, www.cdi.org, www.fas.org.

Every year global population increases by about 76 million people. Is this growth sustainable? *The Population Explosion, Eco-Economy*, www.popplanet.org, www.population-awareness.net, www.familyplanet.org.

Italic=Book Title

Attachment C. Which Guest Speakers Would You Like for the Semester?

Please mark which guest speakers would you like for the semester:
1=yes, 2=no.

1. Alice Paul House, shelter for battered and abused women
2. Senator Allen Kukarich, Westmoreland County, advocate for the poor
3. Don Remig, Even Start, a program working with low-income parents and infants
4. Linda Rudy, Head Start, a preschool program to prepare poor children for elementary school   ·
5. Sarah Steelman (Democrat), House of Representatives, State of Pennsylvania
6. Sam Smith (Republican), House of Representatives, State of Pennsylvania
7. Linda Shaffer, New Choices, which assists single parents, displaced homemakers, and single pregnant women with career development services
8. Barry Shutt, Director, Pennsylvania Bureau of Donated Foods
9. Dennis Darling, Director, Pennsylvania Community Empowerment Office
10. Berry Friesen, Pennsylvania Hunger Action Center, a nonprofit organization dedicated to eliminating the causes of hunger through advocacy, education, and self-sufficiency programs
11. Indiana Housing Authority, low-income housing, Indiana County
12. Habitat for Humanity, which seeks to eliminate inadequate housing. A family that has received a Habitat house can speak.
13. Family Health Council, which administers the WIC (Women, Infants, and Children) program, providing nutrition education and supplemental food for pregnant and nursing women and children age five years and under. Also provides family planning, gynecological care, maternal and childcare, and other services.
14. Vicky Stelma, adult literacy
15. Christopher Martin, Regional Administrator, U.S. Department of Agriculture, Food and Nutrition Services

References

Jonassen, David, Kyle Peck, and Brent Wilson. (1999). "Learning by Reflecting with Technology: Mindtools for Critical Thinking." In *Learning with Technology*, 151-191. Upper Saddle River, NJ: Merrill, Prentice Hall.

U.S. Conference of Mayors. (December 12, 2001). "Hunger and Homeless up Sharply in Major U.S. Cities." http:usmayors.org/uscm/news/press_release/document/hunger.

U.S. Department of Agriculture. (February 24, 1999). "The Second Food Security Measurement and Research Conference." www.ERS.USDA.gov/briefing/foodsecurity/.

Improving the Quality of Hospitality Education Through Service-Learning

by Raphael R. Kavanaugh

Higher education continues to undergo significant changes in order to balance academic excellence with effective strategies for recruiting and retaining students. In an effort to compare the relative merits of academic programs, students and their parents review national rankings and the price/value relationships of programs. However, the overriding issue in the minds of parents and students is often, "Which school will provide the best possible preparation for a chosen career?" Hospitality and tourism management programs are charged with presenting the theory underlying a fundamental understanding of the field, along with developing skills like leadership, communication, research, and a host of "life skills" that enable students to apply the theories they have learned to the situations they will face throughout their lives.

Beyond providing preparation for a specific career, higher education has historically prepared the "total person" through required courses in the humanities, sciences, mathematics, social studies, and composition. This liberal-arts emphasis complements career preparation to create a person ready to function fully in the world of work and in society as a responsible, contributing citizen.

Service-learning allows higher education to facilitate opportunities for students to apply knowledge and experiences gained through their academic preparation to real-world issues. This connection of professional preparation with the social and economic issues confronted by the community brings the learning experiences into sharp focus within the context of career interests. Students receive an opportunity to recognize the importance of improving the quality of life for those less fortunate than they, realize their own potential as problem-solvers, and appreciate their role as active citizens. The American Association for Higher Education (AAHE), in its website, defines service-learning as

> the academically rigorous process of linking course curricula to student engagement in the real-world problems and needs within our communities. This intellectual and civic engagement of students and faculty helps institutions of higher learning bring their scholarly resources to bear on the community needs, as well as assist students in experiencing the relevance of classroom instructions.

The hospitality and tourism industry has a long history of strong support for communities in which its businesses operate. Service coupled with learning creates benefits for students and the community. It has the potential to be a strong educational tool for students and an organization's employees, but this can happen only if the service project is tied directly to the subject content, in a connection between content and activities that must be made continuously. Service-learning experience enhances learning not only by students but by those in-service professionals who see themselves and their employers as contributing importantly to their community. An additional outcome, typically, is increased goodwill among the community members, the university, and the place of business. Finally, students learn, and our industry is reminded, that hospitality and tourism businesses must be caring corporate citizens.

Planned activities in the community tied to a specific set of course or business objectives can profoundly affect a community as well as service providers. But there are some things for which one cannot plan. Our industry can demonstrate human compassion, at its best, when a disaster strikes. The Oklahoma City bombing in 1995 serves as a powerful example of how we can all find ways to serve our communities and enhance the educational experiences of our students. The following account is based on information provided by Debra Bailey of the Oklahoma Restaurant Association.

Case Study: The Oklahoma City Bombing

A bomb exploded in front of the Alfred P. Murrah Federal Building in Oklahoma City on Wednesday, April 19, 1995, at 9:02 am. The explosion rocked the entire downtown area, including the convention center four blocks away, where exhibitors were preparing to continue the Oklahoma Restaurant Association's Foodservice (ORA) Show. More than 430 foodservice vendors were set up to greet approximately 10,000 show attendees, when the impact of the explosion brought the convention to a halt. Suddenly, purveyors and members turned their attention away from meeting new customers and toward serving the needs of victims' families and disaster-relief workers. They found themselves providing a service to the citizens of Oklahoma.

There was so much confusion in those first few minutes that, at first, no one could comprehend the seriousness of what had happened. Shortly after 10 am, a call from the fire marshal's office asked for relief assistance. Within minutes the exhibitors and the show chairman unanimously agreed to forget business and instead direct all their efforts to offer sanctuary to the thousands of displaced workers pouring out of downtown office buildings and to the hundreds of rescue volunteers converging on the bomb site.

Within minutes, equipment and food were being pulled from booths across the exhibit floor. Cold sandwiches, snacks, and beverages were prepared and shuttled to the blast site. The ORA members set up food stations around the Murrah Building, serving the rescuers as they came in and out of the devastated ruins. More calls for help came in for food to sustain not only the rescue effort but the families waiting for news of loved ones at nearby churches and the thousands waiting in line to give blood and help. More than 20,000 hot and cold meals were provided the first day. Refreshments were provided throughout the night.

So many people began pouring into downtown that the FBI had to post guards around the Murrah Building and at the convention center for crowd control. Eventually, some 240 volunteers were assigned to assist daily with the food preparation, cleaning, and service needs. A special concern regarding food safety emerged as individuals brought food prepared in their homes to distribute along the street. Since, from a food safety and sanitation standpoint, some of this food was potentially unsafe, the authorities asked workers to eat only food served by the ORA. City health officials and ORA members patrolled the area and closed down all unauthorized food outlets.

The Federal Emergency Management Agency (FEMA) sent its first teams into Oklahoma City quickly. A call went out for bedding and other supplies to accommodate rescuers at the convention center. Blankets, pillows, and toiletries poured into the convention hall — right down to mints on the pillows. On Thursday morning, April 20, a decision was made to set up MASH units around the blast site. Oklahoma Gas and Electric (OG&E), one of the convention's vendors, moved tons of equipment into the convention center to support the effort there and at a command post established closer to the Murrah Building. In less than ideal conditions, ORA members and vendors provided safe, high-quality food and beverages in a smiling, supportive manner. After the second day, students at the School of Hotel and Restaurant Administration at Oklahoma State University offered to provide relief to the tiring restaurant association volunteers. A faculty member drove a van with eight students to Oklahoma City (a one hour trip) every day for the remainder of the effort. Students and faculty relieved volunteer workers from midnight to 8 am, providing assistance with both food preparation and cleanup. Their efforts made possible 24-hour foodservice for the relief workers.

Over the next 10 days, the ORA, in cooperation with the fire marshal's office, the Health Department, the Governor's Office, FEMA, and the FBI, coordinated the disaster relief effort at the convention center. More than 10 FEMA teams from across the nation were housed and fed at a multi-agency command post in the convention center. As needs were identified, local radio stations would broadcast messages for help. Often far more supplies arrived than were needed. The ORA vendors and restaurateurs kept a steady flow of food pouring into the convention center and the outposts — approximately 15,000 hot and healthy meals each day. More and more emphasis was put on cleanliness and sanitation. Critical time and temperature checks were established and monitored. Temp sticks, gloves, and other supplies were available everywhere to ensure quality and food safety. Still the relief effort continued to grow. Corporate pizza chains set up units to assist, one of them located in the convention center and another at the base of the Murrah Building. Decontamination units were established around the perimeter of the blast site. Foodservice volunteers worked closely with rescuers to provide a comfortable, safe environment for eating and resting. As security tightened, UPS trucks became the "official" carrier of food and supplies into and out of the area. Other services — optical, veterinary, free long-distance phones, mobile phones — were provided as the need arose. On the tenth day following the bombing, the ORA turned the relief operation over to the Red Cross. Since, however, state officials requested that the hot meals continue, school foodservice workers maintained their schedule and worked with the Red Cross. After two long weeks, the rescue effort ceased and the healing began.

Dubbed the "Oklahoma Standard," the relief effort led by the ORA foodservice and hospitality professionals has dramatically influenced federal disaster programs. FEMA and other federal agencies now realize the effectiveness of coordinating their work with the association community. Other associations offered their expertise and assistance. For example, when the search dog's feet were cut on the building debris, the veterinary association was solicited for support. The Hotel/Motel Association provided much of the bedding and toiletry supplies. The Nurses Association, the Insurance Association, and many other professional organizations came forward to assist as well. During the weeks following the disaster, "success by association" took on a whole new meaning in Oklahoma and indeed across the country.

The Oklahoma Restaurant Association was in the right place at the right time, and forged strong relationships with city, state, and federal officials as well as with its own vendors. The ORA members hope they never have to go through anything like this again, but it was a blessing to have been able to help when the time came. As for the 64 students who participated in the midnight to 8 am relief shift over that eight-day period, it is hard to imagine the lessons they learned. They had a unique opportunity to participate in an amazing recovery effort following a national tragedy. Many of them reported that it was the most significant event in their college careers.

Conclusion

Few students will be called to act as did so many in Oklahoma City. Nevertheless, those tragic days remind us that creating service-learning activities that enable students to apply their knowledge to vital societal needs is both an important learning opportunity and an academic responsibility. There are many effective examples of how hospitality educators across our discipline can involve their students in meaningful community service while providing a higher quality of education.

Hospitality and tourism educators have an opportunity, even a responsibility, to incorporate service-learning activities into the curriculum. The addition of required service-learning makes a strong statement about the values we place on our skills and our communities. As a past president of the International Council on Hotel, Restaurant and Institutional Education (I-CHRIE), I encourage the organization's leaders to work to incorporate service-learning as an element of curriculum evaluation for programs seeking accreditation through the Accreditation Commission for Programs in Hospitality Administration (ACPHA). I also urge them to continue to support the activities of the Service-Learning Special Interest Group by providing time at annual conferences to organize presentations that advance knowledge of service-learning theory and practice among the general membership. Articles about service-learning and its benefits published in our academic journals represent another excellent vehicle to advance this knowledge. I suggest that "special issues" be devoted to service-learning, its educational impact and benefit to the community.

Speaking as the head of an academic department of hospitality and tourism management, I also encourage all in academic leadership positions in colleges and universities to support the incorporation of service-learning activities at appropriate places in their programs. And when these activities take place, I encourage academic leaders to be sure to acknowledge faculty for their efforts. Each service-learning activity represents an excellent opportunity to publicly promote one's program, faculty, students, and our industry in general for their commitment to the common good.

I challenge my colleagues to consider service-learning as a vehicle to stimulate economic development — an ambitious strategy to promote the well-being of our communities. It can even be argued that serving the common good includes lessons about the free-market economy, as for-profit enterprises engage in community betterment activities. Oklahoma City is a case in point. Were it not for the success of the businesses at the conference, those organizations would not have been in the financial position to provide products and services in their community's time of need.

Afterword: Food for Thought About the Industry That Cares

by Joseph Koppel

In the Introduction to this volume, I briefly traced how Ellsworth Statler helped establish a tradition of industry support for hospitality education. However, that was not the only philanthropic tradition he helped establish. Another notable tradition practiced by the Statler hotels — and their subsequent owners, the Hilton Hotels — involved making a significant financial contribution to a local community organization upon the opening of each new hotel. This practice represents only one example of how the hospitality industry has repeatedly demonstrated concern not only for the bottom line but also for the welfare of the community.

In their article "Hospitality with a Heart," DeFranco and Kripner (1997) identify numerous lodging and foodservice companies that assist community-based organizations with hunger and shelter issues. Such assistance goes back at least as far as the Great Depression, when many restaurants used their special training to help those in need. Similarly, in "Doing Well by Doing Good," Elizabeth Johnson (1999) identifies a number of hoteliers that provide shelter and other services to meet community needs. She notes how the Grand Hyatt Atlanta's commitment to year-around initiatives results in "making [employees] feel good about the place [they] work, and that means a lot in today's labor market." In this regard, Johnson cites *Good Company: Caring as Fiercely as You Compete,* in which Diane McFerrin remarks, "Companies have the right to expect the very best from their employees, but only when they create an environment worthy of it. People will never care because they have to, but they want to. And then it's magic." Space makes it impossible to identify here more than a few representative industry programs. We begin with Darden Restaurants, which offers casual dining at approximately 1,000 units, primarily Red Lobster and Olive Garden locations. The company's philanthropic giving includes support for education and social services. Explaining why community involvement is so important, Chairman and CEO Joe R. Lee noted in 2002:

> We believe community involvement is part of our civic rent. When guests dine in our restaurants, they are buying more than a great meal, they are also "buying" our ethics, it's the way you do business when you intend to be the best company in the casual dining industry, now and for generations. We believe being a good neighbor and giving back to our communities is critical to our success. (Lee 2002)

That the largest hotel on the West Coast, the San Francisco Hilton, feels similarly about its social responsibility can be gleaned from the fact it created a new position related to service. In 1995, vice-president and general manager Holger Gantz appointed Jo Licata to the full-time position of community projects manager. Here is the logic for this move:

> A hotel and/or a restaurant are not an island existing in isolation. Your neighbors are the businesses, schools and agencies, which form the community where you do business . . . where your customers visit . . . where you and your employees live. Social issues such as clean streets, crime abatement, homelessness, and community economic development have a profound impact on your ability to do business and to be successful. If you are not a part of the effort to improve the economic life and vitality of your community, you will certainly have a difficult time sustaining a thriving business. Only by building the collaborations between our industry, education and the community organizations can we hope to survive and grow. (Gantz and Licata 2002)

Such a statement cannot help but recall a point Drucker (1955) made in his classic text, *The Practice of Management:*

> What is most important is that management realizes that it must consider the impact of every business policy and business action upon society. It has to consider whether the action is likely to promote the public good, to advance the basic beliefs of our society, to contribute to stability, strength, and harmony.

The San Francisco Hilton program, among its many activities, matches hotel surplus supplies and equipment with non-profit needs. This has evolved into the San Francisco Hotel Non-Profit Collaborative, a hospitality-industry recycling and reuse network. At one of its recent monthly meetings, I watched local community-based organizations work face-to-face with hotel, restaurant, and industry suppliers to identify needs and available resources. Indeed, it has been reported by Licata that, over the years, the Hilton San Francisco has diverted approximately 800 tons of material, equipment, foods, and supplies from the waste stream to the local community. It is only natural that students from the University of San Francisco's hospitality management program have begun working with this collaborative as a part of their service-learning. Licata confirmed this involvement at the collaborative's meeting of July 11, 2002.

Our third example features an independent restaurant in Philadelphia. According to its website, the White Dog Café has, during the last 18 years, become nationally known and valued for its leadership in social and environmental activism, as well as its good cooking. Owner Judy Wicks found a way to merge her love for inventive cuisine, social activism, and practical business. In a sense, her establishment provides haute cuisine for the soul as well as the body. According to *Condé Nast Traveler,* her award-winning establishment can be said "to use food to lure innocent customers into social activism" (See www.whitedog.com). Here is a sampling of its community activities.

The Philadelphia Sister Restaurant Project helps publicize minority-owned restaurants that feature minority cultural attractions. Another program, started in 1992, provides mentoring opportunities for students in the Restaurant, Hotel and Tourism Academy at West Philadelphia High School. Participating youngsters gain workplace and community service experience, take field trips to suppliers and farms, and enjoy both recreational and cultural activities. Each year a culinary scholarship of $1,000 is awarded to a graduate of the program to attend one of the restaurant's hospitality educational programs. The Child Watch Visitation Program, conceived of by the Children's Defense Fund, allows the café to help its customers experience first-hand the lives of inner-city children. The program begins at the café with breakfast and a speaker. Philadelphia Citizens for Children and Youth then conducts visits to child- and family-serving facilities such as schools, public health centers, general detention centers, shelters, and recreation centers.

In contrast to the efforts of this small independent restaurant, we have one of the world's leading hospitality companies, the Marriott Corporation, which operates more than 1,800 units in United States and 52 other countries and territories. In 1999, Marriott became the first company of its kind to commit to Gen. Colin Powell's outreach efforts as chair of America's Promises — The Alliance for Youth. Powell praised Marriott's Spirit to Serve Our Communities initiative, a partnership that links the corporation to groups such as the National Urban League, Junior Achievement, and the National Academy Foundation. Other current Spirit to Serve initiatives include:

• Pathways to Independence, providing training jobs for public-assistance recipients

• Career Opportunities Fund, offering $100,000 in grants annually to students and at-risk youth

• Bridges . . . From School to Work, encouraging and training businesses to employ high school students with disabilities (sponsored by the Marriott Foundation for People with Disabilities)

• Family services, offering $100,000 in grants annually to organizations that provide child care, legal assistance, literacy training, and other work and life services

• Support for Habitat for Humanity, providing volunteers and $80,000 annually to build homes in cities where Marriott has large meetings

• Support for America's Second Harvest, helping associates give their time to conduct food drives, work at food banks sorting and packaging food, and volunteer at agencies serving the hungry

According to *Green Hotelier* (Fletcher 2002), the magazine of the International Hotels Environmental Initiative, during the past decade, "Marriott has stepped forward as an industry leader to advance the environmental agenda. By implementing a wide range of environmental solutions across its hospitality portfolio, the Company intends to increase its efforts every year to conserve and protect global natural resources." Ed Fuller, president and managing director of Marriott-International Lodging, confirmed this progressive attitude elsewhere in the magazine: "I believe that industry leaders are becoming increasingly aware of the value of sustainable business practices. We will begin to see these practices incorporated into business plans and become standard operating procedures in the next five to ten years. . . . These practices will go from being a 'nice thing to do' to becoming a business imperative."

Our last example of the industry's commitment to community service is Sodexho, with nearly $5 billion in annual contract-feeding sales in North America. Michel Landel, the corporation's president and CEO, has issued the following statement:

> We are deeply committed to being a driving and creative force that contributes to a hunger-free nation. Improving the quality of daily life defines the Sodexho culture. But we provide more than food service and facilities management. We respond to the needs of the communities. Our initiatives include:
> • Children's food, nutrition and mentoring programs.
> • Culinary job skills training to help break the cycle of poverty.
> • Encouraging and supporting Sodexho employees' spirit of service in support of hunger related initiatives in their communities.
> (Landel n.d.)

Sodexho was recognized in 2001 as Grand Winner of the William D. Littleford Award for Corporate Community Service. This honor was developed by the editors of *American Business Media* to recognize organizations dedicated to helping their local community and society in general.

Not only individual companies but industry leadership organizations have established a strong track record of community involvement. The American Hotel and Lodging Association, for example, is also an active partner in America's Promise, while the National

Restaurant Association runs a joint program with the U.S. Department of Agriculture that makes food available to community organizations across the country. The growing visibility of social responsibility programs like these suggests that students with service-learning experience would likely improve their chance of being hired by companies with clear social values. Indeed, Stephen O'Connor (2002) of Marriott's university relations and property staffing makes this very point:

> *During our recruitment presentations to students we talk about our culture and history. We talk about how we encourage community involvement by our associates and we emphasize how important it is to return to the community, in which we live and work. In a case where our assessment of multiple students is equal or similar, we would give greater consideration to an individual with demonstrated community involvement.*

Stacey Leigh Hoffner (2002), university-relations manager of Red Lobster, has staked out a similar position:

> *Darden seeks employees who understand that the health of a community is directly tied to the health of our business. We want to be of service to our communities just as we want to be of service to our guests. One of the keys to our business has always been finding great leaders to lead our restaurant teams. Community services activities help develop leadership skills — the skills that are required to be a successful leader in our industry.*

Statements like these send a strong and clear message to hospitality educators about the importance of community involvement as modeled by our industry partners. The rationale that industry leaders offer for their community involvement, as well as their indications of what they look for in new employees, should lead educators to consider service-learning one of their potentially most important teaching-learning strategies.

Here is some food for thought. The editors of this volume have sought to demonstrate how *both* hospitality educators and hospitality industry leaders are contributing to the greater community and working toward the common good. Why, then, are these two groups are not working more in common? We have an opportunity to extend two strong traditions and to achieve even more than we can independently. It is, in short, time for the International Council on Hotel, Restaurant and Institutional Education (I-CHRIE) to seek a new type of partnership with our industry colleagues. It is time for us to become true Partners in Service.

We could devise a change model for such a partnership by drawing upon the ideas in Kotter's "Leading Change" (1995). This would involve I-CHRIE's adoption of several concrete strategies.

1. **Establishing a Sense of Urgency.** Meetings of I-CHRIE's Special Interest Group for Service-Learning are now attended by only a handful of members. We need to cooperate aggressively to become more effective. Educators and industry leaders need to share their service efforts to the community with other in-service programs. I-CHRIE must recognize the value of the teaching method of service-learning. A resounding endorsement from the leaders will make change more achievable. With a primary, although not exclusive, focus on social issues related to hunger and homelessness, hospitality education and the hospitality industry can have a far greater impact on these issues by working together.

2. **Forming a Powerful Guiding Coalition.** I-CHRIE's Special Interest Group on Service-Learning could provide leadership, but a more permanent and central commitment to service-learning must be articulated in the organization's guiding vision. Further, the authors of this volume need to advocate for more efforts by their colleagues, fellow members, and industry partners. I-CHRIE's representatives to the industry associations should extend a formal invitation to join in our community engagement efforts.

3. **Creating a Vision.** We need to articulate a clear statement about the nature of service-learning for our educator members and our industry partners. We should also consider the benefits of working with our industry as Partners in Service for the common good, and should develop strategies as to what educators can bring to business projects and what business partners can bring to educators. This vision should also include concurrent strategies to develop more service-learning practitioners among our members. We should offer preconference workshops, with industry representatives invited.

4. **Communicating the Vision.** We need more "print" for our vision. The present volume represents an excellent start, but we need to hear more about how educators and members of industry are working within their communities. Members should be asked to refer to their own institution's mission for reference to service to community and other means of civic engagement. Our leaders should support this move-

ment in education through I-CHRIE's print material and other media. They must lead the change by supporting and practicing service-learning. Educators and members of industry need to be better informed about each other's community engagement activities. Co-authoring articles or co-presenting at conferences could help meet this need.

5. **Empowering Others to Act on the Vision.** Educators, following the practice of industry leaders, must embrace the idea that we teach respect for more than just bottom-line results. Embracing a broader set of goals that include civic engagement should be linked to embracing a broader set of teaching-learning strategies. Service-learning should be recognized as especially useful to our work, and should be formally endorsed by I-CHRIE and reflected in the association's accreditation standards. Service-learning should be encouraged as a teaching method, within our accreditation program evaluations, and as a meaningful way to serve our communities.

6. **Creating Short-Term Wins.** We have already enjoyed one major achievement through receiving financial support from our industry partners to fund this publication. We now need to create other resources like conference workshops that can develop the service-learning skills of members. At future conferences, a general assembly session should be devoted to the benefits of service-learning as a teaching method and the potential of the Partners in Service. We also need to recognize and reward members involved in service-learning practice, including model collaborations between education and industry. Such awards would send a powerful message to all involved in hospitality programs.

7. **Consolidating Improvements and Producing Still More Change.** Within I-CHRIE's service-learning special interest group, we should establish an advisory committee that would report to the association's board of directors on activities in this area. The group would also meet at the annual conference to develop and identify new goals and projects. The completion of our monograph is but the first step in a long journey to integrate service-learning into hospitality education.

8. **Institutionalizing New Approaches.** We should explain our successful connections, as educators, industry leaders, and Partners in Service, to the full membership of both groups and to the new leaders of I-CHRIE each year. This would

demonstrate how the teaching method has helped improve our learning outcomes and service responsibilities.

In conclusion, this monograph can be seen as a single, complex call for hospitality education and the hospitality industry to recommit themselves to the Statler philosophy. The service efforts by industry leaders and educators have demonstrated the tremendous potential of service-learning and the way in which it reflects the best in our hospitable traditions. Hospitality educators have long relished the bounty of our world as represented by food, beverages, lodging, and travel. It is a good life we help to create and a good life most of us enjoy. But as the nearly two dozen volumes in the American Association for Higher Education service-learning series make vividly clear, more effective delivery of learning and more meaningful community engagement are ideas whose time has come. Hospitality educators should, of course, be among our natural leaders in promoting such developments, for they are intrinsic to our tradition of caring for others. We invite industry to join us as Partners in Service, committed to making more of a difference in our communities.

Never doubt that a small group of thoughtful, committed citizens can change the world; indeed, it is the only thing that ever has.
— Margaret Mead

References

DeFranco, Agnes, and Olga Kripner. (1997). "Hospitality with a Heart — A Choice for Success." *Journal of Hospitality & Tourism Education* 9 (1): 5-11.

Drucker, Peter. (1955). *The Practice of Management.* New York: Harper & Row.

Fletcher, Karen. (May 2002). "International Hotels Environment Imitative — A Review of Progress." *Green Hotelier* 25: 32 and 26: 33.

Gantz, Holger, and Jo Licata. (Aug. 26, 2002). Email.

Hoffner, Stacey Leigh. (Oct. 22, 2002). Email.

Johnson, Elizabeth. (Dec. 1999). "Doing Well by Doing Good." *Lodging*: 41.

Kotter, John P. (March-April 1995). "Leading Change: Why Transformation Efforts Fail." *Harvard Business Review*: 59-67.

Landel, Michael. (n.d.). "Hunger Has Serious Side Effects." www.stop-hunger.org.

Lee, Joe R. (2002). www.dardenrestaurants.com

O'Connor, Stephen. (Sept. 16, 2002). Email.

Annotated Bibliography: Service-Learning Resources for the Hospitality Educator

by Keith H. Mandabach

Ackerman, M., and F. Berger. (1994). "Community Service and the Hospitality Curriculum." *Cornell Quarterly* 35 (4): 86-95.

This article describes student activities in a required human-relations course at Cornell's School of Hotel Administration. Students were formed into groups and assigned the responsibility of "volunteering" in a local human-services agency. They were given the opportunity to choose their assignments, which included visiting with residents in nursing homes, serving in soup kitchens, and tutoring at-risk children. The students learned first-hand the effect of cutbacks in government programs for the disadvantaged. The article describes student perspectives and reflections on their participation in the project. Students felt the interpersonal interaction was very positive and that volunteerism is important. The article also makes a case for mandatory service-learning, because when not required to students did not continue volunteer assignments in subsequent semesters.

Brundy, J.L. (1990). *Fostering Volunteer Programs in the Public Sector.* San Francisco, CA: Jossey-Bass Inc.

This well-written, sometimes humorous book chronicles approaches to fostering volunteer programs in the public sector. It provides examples of research about volunteer perceptions of volunteering in government projects, and offers suggestions for organizing a volunteer program. These include organizing the program, matching volunteers and community needs, educating constituents for volunteer service, training them for volunteer activities, and evaluating and recognizing the volunteers. The book offers some interesting ideas for service-learning opportunities for those in the hospitality industry.

Clark, S.C. (2000). "The More We Serve, the More We Learn: Service-Learning in a Human Resource Management Course." In *Working for the Common Good. AAHE Management Service Learning Monographs.* Edited by Paul Godfrey and Edward Grasso, 143-147. Washington, DC: AAHE.

Sue Campbell Clark's article describes service-learning human resource consulting projects required in a class at the University of Idaho. The article offers suggestions for forming student service-learning work groups, identifying potential organizations to serve, project development, project reports, reflections, and evaluations. The author describes the synergy that results from student participation in service-learning. Or, as the author says, "the more we serve, the more we learn."

Conners, T.D. (1995). *The Volunteer Management Handbook*. New York: John Wiley & Sons, Inc.

This very structured book is a detailed how-to on creating a volunteer program that might assist those developing a service-learning program. The best of the organizational strategies are the sections on training volunteers. Sections on policy development and legal issues involving volunteering are especially applicable to those in educational service-learning programs.

Coplin, W. D. (2000). *How You Can Help*. New York: Rutledge.

This is a self-help textbook that is designed for "do-gooders." This is a label the author cheerfully accepts as if it were an honor badge. The book is written in a comfortable how-to format that makes for easy reading. After discussing the "blessing and the curse of Mother Teresa," parts one and two provide purpose and definition to volunteering. The next section proposes service projects for all walks of society: families, neighbors, employees, consumers, investors, social organizations, retirees, students, and alumni. In my opinion, the book's greatest relevance to the academy (most of us exist in the organized anarchy of institutional decision making) is its final section on cooperative problem solving.

Cyrs, T.E., and E. Conway. (1997). *Teaching at a Distance with the Merging Technologies: An Instructional Research Approach*. Las Cruces, NM: Center for Educational Development, New Mexico State University.

Thomas Cyrs and Eugenia Conway are dedicated teachers and trainers. Their book focuses on distance education and discusses the background of distance education: planning and organizing it, producing and presenting the courses, course administration, and course evaluation. While the lessons are designed to improve distance education, many of the suggestions are also extremely relevant to the service-learning delivery system of education.

Service-learning often occurs in off-campus locations and, like distance education, requires a comprehensive plan for success. All teachers can learn from the suggestions Cyrs and Conway present to make the educational process "good television." The most interesting chapter presents methods for using trigger videos to stimulate higher-order learning.

Crosby, M.A. (1994). "A History of Helping Hands," *Restaurants USA* 11 (8): 35- 38.

This article briefly chronicles the American restaurant industry's history of community service. The article recounts how Lorenzo Delmonico of Delmonico's Restaurant managed New York City's efforts to feed the unfortunate during the Panic of 1873, and how this heritage led the National Restaurant Association to include a code of ethics in its national bylaws when it was formed in 1922. The article recounts numerous episodes of restaurateurs around the country assisting those in need, including feeding the hungry during the Depression, assisting the Red Cross during World War II, and supporting the creation of the Ronald McDonald House and Share our Strength programs.

DeFranco, A.L., and O.M. Kripner. (1997). "Hospitality with a Heart — A Choice for Success." *Journal of Hospitality & Tourism Education* 9 (1): 5-10.

This article documents a program at the University of Houston, Hilton College, designed to train the homeless for work in the hospitality industry. The article also includes a list of resource organizations, many active on national and local levels. After briefly defining issues involved with the homeless, the article traces the hospitality industry's history of community outreach. In addition to the public-service reasons for getting involved in community service, the authors stress the economic benefits for those considering such a project. The article describes three successful projects involving the homeless. It shows that effective use of a shelter agency through the support of a dedicated case manager enabled the hospitality industry to provide employment options to those who would otherwise have few opportunities. The article also includes an appendix that details the step-by-step processes of the CHOICE program.

Dev, C.S. (1990). "Measuring the Value of Experiential Learning." *Cornell Quarterly* 31 (2):105-107.

Dev describes an experiential learning component of a marketing class at Cornell University. Students were assigned marketing projects for off-campus businesses. The article describes the analysis of questionnaire results conducted after the project. Students and clients deemed the experiential approach a valuable educational technique.

Dewey, J. (1915). *Democracy in Education*. New York: Simon & Schuster.

Dewey's classic needs no introduction but is a must in this bibliography because of his pioneer work in promoting experiential and service-leaning education. Dewey describes the personal experiences that contributed to the development of his philosophy of education. He presents a variety of educational perspectives and promotes the importance of educators developing theories and foundations based on their experience and educational philosophies. The progressive spirit of the book may appear dated to some, but it is always refreshing.

Eyler, J., D.E. Giles, and A. Schmiede. (1996). *A Practitioner's Guide to Reflection in Service-Learning: Student Voices and Reflection*. Nashville, TN: Vanderbilt University Press.

This is a workbook-based resource that describes student experiences and critical reflection on service-learning experiences. It seeks to develop reflective activities in service-learning and is based on student comments. Providing content suggestions and ideas for using service-learning in a wide variety of programs, it emphasizes what students feel is important. It also discusses the importance of a multi-dimensional approach that encompass a wide variety of learning styles.

Eyster, J., J. Ford, and A. Hales. (1988). "Housing and Feeding the Homeless: Applying Hospitality Expertise to Public Service." *Cornell Quarterly* 29 (2): 71-75.

This article describes a pioneer service-learning effort designed by Cornell's hotel and restaurant management program to provide valuable consulting resources for agencies that feed and house the homeless. In addition to working with local agencies, it brought students to Washington, DC, to apply expertise to human-service agencies in food and equipment purchasing, upkeep, and sanitation. The article stresses the fact that students felt the project connected them to the human side of the hospitality industry and provided hands-on experience while solving real issues.

Eyster, J., J. Ford, and A. Hales. (1991). "Making a Difference: How You and Your Hotel Can Creatively Assist the Hungry and Homeless in Your Community." *Cornell Quarterly* 32 (1): 101-104.

This article details the continuation of the service-learning program outlined in the 1988 article described above. It explains how Cornell University's HRI programs returned to Washington, DC, to contribute expertise to local human-service organizations that serve the hungry and homeless. It describes a consultant project, explaining how to operate a shelter for the homeless, and suggests that soup kitchens piggyback their food orders onto industry participants, thus gaining the pricing advantages enjoyed by high-volume purchasers. The *Cornell Quarterly* grants anyone permission to copy the article. The authors encourage hospitality educators to join their effort to make a difference by improving efforts to help the homeless.

Frankenna, W. (1965). *Philosophy of Education.* New York: McMillan.

Frankenna provides a framework for development of a value-based philosophy of education. He presents his ideas on education along with a thoughtful interpretation of John Dewey's and Jacques Maritain's philosophies of education and their support of experiential education.

Hales, A. (1992). "Beyond Homeless Shelters and Soup Lines: Update from a Washington, D.C., Shelter." *Cornell Quarterly* 33 (4): 77-79.

This article describes the efforts by a team of food and beverage experts and other volunteers, from Cornell University and the Ithaca community, in 1991, to support the Community for Creative Non-Violence. This is a shelter that provides meals and accommodations for some 1,400 homeless people in Washington, DC. In a 1987 visit, a Cornell team had instructed shelter volunteers in how to use commercial kitchen equipment and to schedule high-volume meals. In the intervening four years, much of that information was lost (as was some of the equipment), and the kitchen itself suffered from deferred maintenance. The 1991 team prepared a consulting report aimed at establishing basic operating policies for sanitation, food preparation, and equipment maintenance. Such visits raise a larger question of what the hospitality industry can do to restructure employment and homeownership possibilities for homeless people.

Jacoby, B., et al. (1996). *Service Learning in Higher Education: Concepts and Practices.* San Francisco, CA: Jossey-Bass.

Targeted for senior administrators, faculty, community leaders, policymakers, and student affairs professionals, this book provides a theoretical framework that places service-learning within the larger realm of the educational outcomes in higher education. It is a resource for those interested in beginning a service-learning program. Of special interest to faculty is the description of how service-learning improves the teaching process.

Johnson, S.O., and S.E. Taranto. (1984). *Educational Volunteerism a New Look.* Springfield, IL: Charles C. Thomas.

This book is designed for teachers and volunteers. While primarily designed for K-12 volunteer and service-learning projects, it offers suggestions for initiating and revising programs that have applications in higher education. The book consists mainly of lists, which provide references that can be used in any volunteer or service-learning program. Especially helpful are the evaluation rubric forms for instructor training and volunteer program effectiveness.

Kendall, J.C., et al. (1990). *Combining Service and Learning: A Resource Book for Community and Public Service.* 3 vols. Raleigh, NC: National Society for Internships and Experiential Education.

This three-volume set is a reference guide. The first volume provides the background and a discussion of educational principles supporting service-learning concepts. The second volume describes examples of service-learning programs, their challenges and successes. The final volume contains a fully indexed, annotated bibliography.

Kim, H. Young. (1999). "Giving a Helping Hand to a Hunger Program: Combining Service-Learning and Managerial Communication Basics." *Journal of Hospitality & Tourism Education* 11 (2/3): 22-25.

The article provides a faculty member's perspective on the service-learning activities of a freshman communication class. The author offers suggestions for maximizing the effectiveness of the limited participation time of individual students in service-learning activities, while maintaining instructional relevance. The class developed publicity materials for the Friendship Domains Network, a local nonprofit organization that accepts and distributes donations to food pantries, after-school programs, social agencies, and soup kitchens in Ithaca, NY. The primary project was developing a public relations program orchestrated through the writing and distribution of press releases. Three positive results were products of the project. Faculty and students learned from and enjoyed working on the project; two of the press releases were actually printed by prestigious national publications; and the students felt the project helped them learn and apply communication skills in a real and immediate context not available in the classroom.

LeBruto, S., and K. Murray. (1994). "The Educational Value of 'Captive Hotels.'" *Cornell Quarterly* 35 (4): 72-79.

The authors identified 12 hotel-management schools that maintain full-service hotels used to provide experiential education to the students in their programs. They investigated the perceived importance of such "captive hotels" in delivering practical hotel-management education. The study measured the perception of the importance of practical education and captive training facilities in developing 10 competencies that hotel-management graduates should possess. This article supports the importance of experiential hospitality education.

Michaelson, L.K., L.D. Fink, and A. Knight. (1996). "What Every Faculty Developer Needs to Know about Learning Groups." In *To Improve the Academy: Resources for Faculty, Instructional and Organizational Development.* Stillwater, OK: New Forums Press.

Michaelson, Fink, and Knight provide a detailed strategy about methods to improve teaching effectiveness through group projects. Although the book is about teaching, the authors' management discipline allows a straightforward presentation without the usual "eduspeak." They contend that today's students struggle to see business organizations in their entirety, because they have difficulty communicating and working effectively with others. They also contend that students have trouble solving unstructured problems. But the book is more than just about teaching using groups. The authors document their experience with service-learning and volunteer projects.

O'Halloran, R., and C. O'Halloran. (1999). "Service-Learning in the Hospitality and Tourism Business Environment." *Journal of Hospitality & Tourism Education* 10 (3): 18-22.

The O'Hallorans capture the spirit and the mission of hospitality service-leaning in this article. Service-learning is described as a "natural methodology to utilize to enhance learning opportunities." Eleven benefits of service-learning are detailed: increased retention, providing quality education, increasing relevancy for students, teaching positive values, empowering students and teachers, inviting student community involvement, teaching job skills, contributing to university outreach efforts, increasing campus community collaboration and partnerships, helping community education, and contributing thousands of hours at service to people in need. The article also describes a process for identifying and developing hospitality service-learning, from goals to project management and evaluation. As an example it profiles a nutrition education service-learning project between the University of Denver and the Denver Public Schools. The article concludes that service-learning is an exciting yet rigorous method to strengthen the tie between hospitality educators and industry practice.

Rainsford, P. (1992). "The Small Business Institute: Hands on Learning." *Cornell Quarterly* 33 (4): 73-76.

The Small Business Institute program at Cornell University is designed to provide students experiential learning opportunities as consultants, under faculty supervision, to small businesses. Students integrate the various educational disciplines such as food and beverage management, human resource management, accounting, and communication, into projects selected by the faculty advisor. The author concludes that students learn to examine a wide range of topics that affect the success or failure of a business. Communication exercises occur both orally and in writing with a wide variety of people, through a dialogue that allows learning and problem solving to occur at a higher level than if the students were learning only in the classroom.

Rhoads, R. A. (1997). *Community Service and Higher Learning: Explorations of the Caring Self.* Albany: State University of New York Press.

Calling for a restructuring of learning in a more caring and democratic form, the author promotes community service as a method of transforming higher education into an "ethic-of care" philosophy. Rhoads researched student perceptions of their service-learning projects and demonstrates how community service offers an encounter between the "self" and the "other." The author conceives of service-learning as "critical community service," a combination of democratic concern for social justice and equality with an ethic of care, which provides benefits for faculty, students, and community.

Rhoads, R.A., and J.P.F. Howard, eds. (1998). *Academic Service-Learning: Pedagogy of Action and Reflection*. San Francisco, CA: Jossey-Bass Inc.

This volume includes descriptions of successful service-learning programs and discussions of issues that faculty and students must consider during the incorporation of service-learning into courses and curricula. Four varied but interesting articles develop pedagogical models describing the integration of academic learning with community service. Kathleen Maas Weigert discusses the relevance of service-learning as an innovative pedagogical model that encourages higher learning. Ira Harkavy and Lee Benson conceptualize service-learning as an effort to "de-platonize" and democratize American higher education. This article and the one by Mea Mendel-Reyes on the interconnections between service-learning and citizenship education will stir the emotions that support the progressive ideas of John Dewey. Jeff Howard develops an innovative pedagogical model capable of transforming teaching and learning practices.

Smith, A., and J.M. La Lopa. (2000). "Teaching Students to Think: How Problem-Based Learning Is Revolutionizing the Classroom." *Chef Educator Today* 1 (1): 25-27.

One of the most advanced teaching methods being used in more and more classrooms and laboratories around the country is problem-based learning (PBL). This article describes how PBL can turn an otherwise boring lecture into a dynamic learning environment. The first part of the article deals with the nature of PBL. The second half is dedicated to an example of how chef Carl Behnke applied PBL in the lecture portion of a quantity food production course he teaches in the Department of Restaurant, Hotel, Institutional, and Tourism Management at Purdue University.

Spears, D., R. Gould, C. Boger, and R. Brannan. (1998). "Joint Ventures between the Classroom and Rural Communities." *Journal of Hospitality & Tourism Education* 10 (3): 33-37.

This article describes active learning while developing rural tourism websites and marketing plans in introductory and senior level tourism classes at Kansas State University. Students received instruction from national experts in the analysis of rural tourism websites and participated in team exercises analyzing sample sites from around the country. After being divided into groups, the students visited selected communities and took on the project of developing tourism sites or marketing plans. A discussion of project outcomes for students, the community, and faculty will be especially interesting to those undertaking web-based service-learning projects.

Stevens, B. (1999). "Fostering Volunteerism: A Course in Managerial Communication and Ethics." *Journal of Hospitality & Tourism Education* 11 (2/3): 50-53.

One of the benefits of service-learning is fostering a student's sense of responsibility and an awareness of ethical issues. This article discusses the service-learning activities of a graduate class in organizational communication. It describes how these activities enhanced the students' communication skills and improved their understanding of organizational behavior in relationship to the community. After briefly outlining the hospitality industry's history of volunteerism, and defining service-learning, the article describes class projects to assist the Red Cross in Ithaca, NY. They involved a computer team, a survey team, a drapery donation team, a public relations team, and a kitchen-supply donation team. The projects constituted a win-win situation for the students, faculty, and Red Cross. Students experienced the reality of working within an organization and developed important communications skills in real public relations activities. In addition, because of funding provided for the project, the teams were able to learn the process of managing a budget.

Taylor, L.E., and M.L. Maas. (1995). *The Education Mall: A 21st Century Learning Concept.* Riverside, CA: Maas, Rao, Taylor and Associates. Available from EDRS.

Maas and Taylor go "outside the box" to present a new model for postsecondary education. They postulate that there are three basic problems with higher education. There is a lack of vision of the direction in which it is moving, and thus no idea of how to contribute effectively to the change process. Second, the decision-making process at educational institutions often produces anarchical results. Finally there is a need for a new model for financing public postsecondary education. They propose assembling, in an "education mall," more than 20 businesses and services, including stores, a small-business incubator, an assessment center, foodservices that meet community needs, a high-tech center that would also be a training center, a fitness center, a conference center, a health center, a dental clinic, and much more, which would offer education while providing services and businesses. An "electronic college" would provide additional connection, on and off campus, for all learning and support services. While service-learning programs are designed to send students into the community, this proposal moves the campus into the community. A major benefit would be to provide educational access to those who, for whatever reason, do not come to a traditional campus.

Service Learning Website Links

The American Association for Higher Education
Service-Learning Project.
http://www.aahe.org/service/srv-lrn.htm.
The site for the American Association for Higher Education Service-Learning Project provides information about an 18-volume series of resources for faculty seeking to explore community-based learning in individual academic disciplines. The site explains AAHE's primary role as a facilitator and resource for those whose work brings them into more direct contact with teaching faculty.

American Association of Community Colleges
Service-Learning Site.
http://www.aacc.nche.edu/initiatives/SERVICE/SL_Bib_web.htm
The American Association of Community Colleges has promoted the value of service-learning to the 1,200 associate's-degree-granting institutions in the United States. The site offers useful links and provides examples of service-learning projects from community colleges.

The American Association for Experiential Education.
http://www.aee.org/
The mission of the Association for Experiential Education is to develop and promote experiential education. It is committed to support professional development, theoretical advancement, and evaluation of experiential education worldwide.

The Big Dummy's Guide to Service Learning.
http://www.fiu.edu/~time4chg/Library/bigdummy.html

As the name indicates, this interactive site, from Florida International University, aims to provide specifics about developing a service-learning program or project. It offers step-by-step plans and common questions (with answers) about service-learning.

Campus Compact.
http://www.compact.org/
National Campus Compact is a national coalition of more than 740 college and university presidents committed to the civic purposes of higher education. Campus Compact promotes community service that develops students' citizenship skills and values, encourages partnerships between campuses and communities, and assists faculty who seek to integrate public and community engagement into their teaching and research.

Campus Compact of New Hampshire.
http://www.compactnh.org/pubs.htm
This branch of Campus Compact features a publication list that includes the "Faculty Guide to Service-Learning." It is an easy site to search for service-learning publications.

Learn and Serve — The Corporation for Community Service.
http://www.learnandserve.org/resources/index.html
This site provides resources and ideas for service-learning projects. While primarily focused on K-12, it offers additional information, including possible funding support, that might interest those in higher education.

The International Partnership for Service-Learning.
http://www.ipsl.org/
This is the site for an organization that has originated, designed, and implemented international and intercultural service-learning programs since 1982. These include undergraduate programs and a master's degree in international service for students from the United States and abroad.

The Michigan Journal for Service Learning.
http://www.umich.edu/~mjcsl/
The Michigan Journal of Community Service-Learning (MJCSL) is a peer-reviewed journal publishing articles by faculty and service-learning educators on research, theory, pedagogy, and related issues.

National Service-Learning Clearinghouse.
http://www.servicelearning.org/

The National Service-Learning Clearinghouse (NSLC) supports four national organizations that launch new support services to the service-learning community. The organizations and their advisors assist the Clearinghouse to identify emerging trends and develop educational materials, as well as serve as consultants in the Clearinghouse's strategic planning for service-learning activities. This is a great site for those just entering the world of service-learning. It includes links to sites discussing 12 different areas of service-learning.

.

Contributors

Nancy Burston
Assistant Director
Human Services Coalition of Tompkins County, Inc.
Aurora Street
Ithaca, NY 14850
(607) 273-8686
nab15@cornell.edu

Ronald P. Cole
Assistant Professor
Hotel, Restaurant & Institutional Management
University of Delaware
Raub Hall
14 West Main Street
Newark, DE 19716
(302) 831-6514
rpc@udel.edu

Susan J. Connery
Director, Feinstein Community Service Center
Johnson & Wales University
8 Abbott Park Place
Providence RI 02903
(401) 598-1265
sconnery@jwu.edu

Pamela R. Cummings
Associate Professor
Hotel, Restaurant & Institutional Management
University of Delaware
Raub Hall
14 West Main Street
Newark, DE 19716
(302) 831-6207
cummings@udel.edu

Cynthia S. Deale
Assistant Professor
Kemmons Wilson School of Hospitality & Resort Management
University of Memphis
140D Fogelman College of Business & Economics
3700 Central Ave.
Memphis TN 38152
(901) 678-5699
cdeale@memphis.edu

Marge Dill
Executive Director
Human Services Coalition of Tompkins County, Inc.
Aurora Street
Ithaca, NY 14850
(607) 273-8686
mfd3@cornell.edu

Dori Finley
Professor
Department of Nutrition and Hospitality Management
East Carolina University
Greenville, NC 27858-4353
(252) 328-4222
FinleyD@mail.ecu.edu

Pamela Holsinger-Fuchs
Director, Student Activities and Service Learning
University of Minnesota, Crookston
Crookston, MN 56716
(218) 281-8505
PHOLSING@mail.crk.umn.edu

Alice E. Kaiser-Drobney
Director
Institute for Community, Service-Learning, and Nonprofit
  Leadership
Slippery Rock University
Robert A Lowry Center
Slippery Rock, PA 16057
(724) 738-CARE
alice.kaiser-drobney@sru.edu

Raphael Kavanaugh
Professor and Head
Department of Hospitality and Tourism Management
Purdue University
106 Stone Hall
West Lafayette, IN 47906
(765) 494-4643
kavanaur@cfs.purdue.edu

Joseph Koppel
Chair, School of Hospitality and Tourism
College of the Bahamas, Nassau
P.O. Box N-4912
Nassau, Bahamas
(242) 323-5804 or 6804
dockoppel@hotmail.com

Keith H. Mandabach
Department of Hotel, Restaurant and Tourism Management
New Mexico State University
Box 30003 MSC 3HRTM
Las Cruces, NM 88003-8003
(505) 646-2879
kmandaba@nmsu.edu

Vern Markey
Assistant Professor
Hospitality and Tourism Management
EML Hall
North Dakota State University
Fargo, ND 58105
(701) 231-8220
Vern.Markey@ndsu.nodak.edu

Corrie Martin
Director
Women's Center
Johnson & Wales University
8 Abbott Park Place
Providence RI 02903
(401) 598-2248
cmartin@jwu.edu

James A. Myers
Director
Center for Multidisciplinary Studies
Rochester Institute of Technology
31 Lomb Memorial Drive
Rochester, NY 14623
(585) 475-2234
j_myers@cast-fc.rit.edu

Therese A. O'Connor
Senior Lecturer
School of Hotel Administration
Cornell University
246 Statler Hall
Ithaca, NY 14850
(607) 255-8388
tao3@cornell.edu

Robert M. O'Halloran
Professor & Director
Kemmons Wilson School of Hospitality & Resort Management
University of Memphis
140D Fogelman College of Business & Economics
Memphis TN 38152
(901) 678-5768
rohallrn@memphis.edu

Stephanie Rainsford
School of Hotel Administration
Cornell University
246 Statler Hall
Ithaca, NY 14850

Nancy Swanger
Assistant Professor
Hotel and Restaurant Administration
Washington State University
Todd Hall, Room 475
PO Box 644742
Pullman, WA 99164-4742
(509) 335-2443
swanger@wsu.edu

Tom Van Dyke
Associate Professor
Department of Hotel, Restaurant & Institutional Management
Indiana University of Pennsylvania
911 South Drive 10 Ackerman Hall
Indiana, PA 15705
(724) 357-3280
tvandyke@iup.edu

Shelley Weaver
Department of Hotel, Restaurant & Institutional Management
Indiana University of Pennsylvania
911 South Drive 10 Ackerman Hall
Indiana, PA 15705
(724) 357-4440
weaver_shelley@hotmail.com

Nancy C. Northrop Wolanski
Assistant Director
Feinstein Community Service Center
Johnson & Wales University
8 Abbott Park Place
Providence, RI 02903
(401) 598-1275
nnorthrop@jwu.edu